The Hearing Ear

Learning to Listen to God

LARRY LEA

Creation House
Altamonte Springs, Florida

Creation House
Strang Communications Company
190 N. Westmonte Drive
Altamonte Springs, FL 32714
(407) 869-5005

First Printing, June 1988
Second Printing, July 1988

Contents

A Personal Message
From Larry Lea

Most of us can point to some specific time and say, "That was the turning point in my life." I certainly can. When I think of my turning point, I remember that day back in 1968 when, for the first time in my life, I heard the voice of God.

I was seventeen years old, and I had lost my mind. Locked inside the psychiatric ward of Mother Frances Hospital in Tyler, Texas, I spent most of the time lying on my bed in a drugged stupor with my eyes rolled back in my head. I thought the lady who cleaned my room was my mother and that the patient across the hall was the doctor.

But one day the horrible mental fog around my brain cleared just long enough for a shining ray of hope to penetrate my senses. Falling to my knees, I prayed the only prayer I knew how to pray. Pleading, weeping, I cried out to God. Over and over, I sobbed out His name: "Jesus! Jesus! Oh, merciful Jesus!"

Suddenly, I heard a voice speak in my spirit: "Now you are My son. You will take My message to this generation. You will be My mouth and My minister." Then the

5

voice told me I could get up and go home.

In less than a week, I walked out of that hospital, and I've sought to walk by that same still, small voice ever since.

In 1978 I reached another turning point in my life. That was the year I answered the highest call of all—the call to pray. As I committed myself wholeheartedly to that call, the Holy Spirit opened up to me wonderful prayer secrets. Since I put those secrets into a book and a tape series called *Could You Not Tarry One Hour?* thousands of people and hundreds of churches have been transformed. Reports continue to filter in from all over the world—including Cuba and the underground church in China. This revelation on prayer is shaking and shaping the body of Christ. Believers everywhere are learning to use the beautifully balanced words of Christ's model prayer in Matthew 6 to talk to God.

But God means for prayer to be more than a monologue where one person does all the talking. Prayer should be a dialogue, a conversation. Prayer is not just asking, seeking and knocking; it's also seeing the door open and receiving your answer. Prayer is more than *you* speaking to *God*; it's also *God* speaking to *you*.

There is another reason why we must hear God. Hearing the voice of God is a matter of *life* or *death*, for God Himself commands: "Incline your *ear*, and come to Me. *Hear*, and your soul shall *live*" (Is. 55:3). It's very simple. If you hear God's voice, you will live; if not, you will die.

Believe me when I warn you that days of desperation and deception are ahead. You will need supernatural wisdom to survive and prosper in a crumbling economy. You will need divine discernment to distinguish the satanic from the supernatural. The paths before you will

6

become so complex, so confusing, you will have to hear God's voice saying, "This is the way; walk ye in it," or you may veer off in the wrong direction and abort God's highest plans and purposes for your life. There is no time to waste. You must begin right now to develop the ears of your spirit so you can hear, recognize and obey God's voice.

In times past God spoke from the outside in; now He speaks from the inside out. God wants to speak to you, but you need the vehicle of prayer, and you need ears that hear. As you develop a praying spirit and hearing ears, God will speak to you. You will become intimately acquainted with His voice and His ways.

Take your next step. As you seek God daily in prayer, ask Him to give you hearing ears. Once you hear His voice, all you have to do is obey!

SECTION ONE

Laying a Foundation for Hearing

CHAPTER ONE

You Can Hear God

Several prominent Christian leaders and I had agreed to meet in the Hilton Hotel at the Dallas-Fort Worth airport for a closed-door, two-day meeting. The topic of our discussion? What key issues will the church be forced to face and answer in the 1990s?

During those twelve intense hours of praying, discussing and baring our hearts to one another, we sensed the pull of a strong, deep current of the Spirit tugging, guiding our thoughts toward one central issue. Wave after wave of conversation crested at this point: Old ways, old methods, old ideas will no longer be repeated with success. Men and movements who insist on riding them out will find themselves dry-docked, shipwrecked or sailing under the wrong flag.

Suddenly a towering wave of truth hit us broadside: A confrontation is coming in the days ahead between religion, which takes account only of natural elements and forces and excludes the supernatural or spiritual, and New Testament Christianity, which believes in a hearing, speaking, power-imparting God who is deeply involved and vitally connected with His people.

11

Hear me well. Tides and currents are shifting. Dangerous shoals and treacherous reefs are lying in wait. New winds are blowing. If the church is to move forward in the flow of God, she must catch the fresh wind of the Spirit. The people of God must set their courses by the unwavering, sure revelation of the Holy Spirit. We must hear and obey what the Spirit is saying to the churches.

Can we talk? Can we be honest and transparent with one another? Are you disheartened because God has been dishonored by His people's low level of living? Are you discontent with religious "systems"? Are you deeply aware of your great debt to God and discouraged by the ineffectiveness of your service? Do you earnestly desire to be empowered and led so that God may receive the maximum good and glory from your life? Then you're the person I'm looking for. I wrote this book to let you know that you can hear and follow the voice of the Lord in your spirit. You—yes, you—can have hearing ears, and I'm going to teach you how to get them.

God Wants You to Have "Hearing Ears"

Several years ago, one of my dear pastor friends said, "Larry, when I was praying for you the other day, I had a vision. In my vision, I saw you with great, big "Mickey Mouse" ears. Everything else about you looked normal except for your enormous, elephant-sized ears. I asked the Lord to tell me what the vision meant and to explain why I saw you with such big ears. The Spirit of the Lord spoke back to me and said: 'Larry Lea has developed his hearing. He has developed his spiritual ears.' "

How about you? Would you like to learn how to develop your spiritual hearing to the point where you have big "Mickey Mouse" ears? Would you like to be able to hear what the Holy Spirit is speaking to your spirit?

12

First, you must understand that it is God's will for you to hear His voice. Just pause a moment and say aloud: "It is God's will for me to hear His voice."

Did you say it? Do you believe it? The Word of God clearly reveals that it is God's will for men and women to hear His voice. Let's take a moment to examine just a few of the many scriptural examples that teach us that God does speak to individuals.

The Old Testament

If you've studied the Bible, you know that you don't have to read far before discovering that God spoke to people in Old Testament times. Old Testament writers record explicit, detailed communication between God and Adam and Eve, Noah, Abraham, Samuel, Isaiah, Jeremiah and many others.

God Spoke to Adam and Eve

And the Lord God commanded the man, saying, "Of every tree of the garden you may freely eat; but of the tree of the knowledge of good and evil you shall not eat, for in the day that you eat of it you shall surely die" (Gen. 2:16-17).

Many people mistakenly believe that God speaks to men and women only through sermons or through some inexpressible spiritual or emotional impulse. But notice that God did not speak to Adam through a preacher or through some vague mystical "impression." No, He communicated directly and verbally with Adam.

You and I know that Adam and Eve's sin cost them the wonderful communion with God that they had enjoyed in the Garden of Eden. But Jesus died for mankind's sin and was resurrected so we could be

13

reconciled to God and once again enjoy communion with Him. (See Rom. 5:17-19; 1 Cor. 15:47-48.)

God Spoke to Noah

Now remember: There were no Bibles, preachers or churches in Noah's day. It was just God and Noah. God spoke to this righteous man who had found favor in His sight, and He spoke clearly and in vivid detail:

> So God looked upon the earth, and indeed it was corrupt; for all flesh had corrupted their way on the earth. And God said to Noah, "The end of all flesh has come before Me, for the earth is filled with violence through them; and behold, I will destroy them with the earth. Make yourself an ark of gopherwood; make rooms in the ark, and cover it inside and outside with pitch.
>
> "And this is how you shall make it; the length of the ark shall be three hundred cubits, its width fifty cubits, and its height thirty cubits. You shall make a window for the ark, and you shall finish it to a cubit from above; and set the door of the ark in its side. You shall make it with lower, second, and third decks" (Gen. 6:12-16).

After God specified exactly how to build the ark, He went on to give instructions regarding Noah's family, the animals, food and so forth. (See Gen. 6:17-7:4.) In order to comprehend why, when and how to build the ark and carry out God's unusual commands, Noah needed specific details, not vague impressions. And God spoke to Noah, giving him the necessary instructions.

God Spoke to Abraham

The book of Genesis records several instances where God gave Abraham wonderful promises and clear-cut instructions. For instance, it was God who commanded Abraham to leave Ur of the Chaldeans and go to Canaan.

> Now the Lord had said to Abram: "Get out of your country, from your kindred and from your father's house, to a land that I will show you. I will make you a great nation; I will bless you and make your name great; and you shall be a blessing. I will bless those who bless you, and I will curse him who curses you; and in you all the families of the earth shall be blessed" (Gen. 12:1-3).

One of the greatest tests of Abraham's life came about many years later when God spoke to him and commanded him to offer his son Isaac as a burnt offering.

> Now it came to pass after these things that God tested Abraham, and said to him, "Abraham!" And he said, "Here I am."
> And He said, "Take now your son, your only son Isaac, whom you love, and go to the land of Moriah, and offer him there as a burnt offering on one of the mountains of which I shall tell you" (Gen. 22:1-2).

As Abraham proceeded to carry out God's instructions, the angel of the Lord, whom I believe to be the preincarnate Christ, spoke to Abraham:

> And Abraham stretched out his hand and took the knife to slay his son. But the Angel of the Lord called to him from heaven and said, "Abraham, Abraham!" And he said, "Here I am."
> And He said, "Do not lay your hand on the lad, or do anything to him; for now I know that you fear God, seeing you have not withheld your son,

15

your only son, from Me."

...Then the Angel of the Lord called to Abraham a second time out of heaven, and said: "By Myself I have sworn, says the Lord, because you have done this thing, and have not withheld your son, your only son, in blessing I will bless you, and in multiplying I will multiply your descendants as the stars of the heaven and as the sand which is on the seashore; and your descendants shall possess the gate of their enemies. In your seed all the nations of the earth shall be blessed, because you have obeyed My voice" (Gen. 22:10-12,15-18).

The reason Abraham could hear God in the crucial times was that he had been hearing and obeying all along. Notice how Abraham immediately obeyed each individual command of the Lord.

When the angel of the Lord commanded, "Don't slay Isaac! I was only testing you to see what was in your heart," Abraham responded immediately. If Abraham had been like a lot of "good charismatics," at that point he probably would have rebuked the "devil" and driven his knife right through Isaac's heart. He would have said, "I've already heard one thing, and I refuse to deviate from what I've already heard." But Abraham had learned to hear, know and obey the voice of God.

God Spoke to Moses

Moses got ahead of God's timing, acted according to human reasoning and made a mess of things. After tending sheep forty years on the backside of the desert, he was resigned to thinking that God's plans and purposes for his life were long since null and void. Although Moses hadn't consciously heard anything from God in a long time, the Lord arranged a divine encounter to get his attention.

> And the Angel of the Lord appeared to him in a flame of fire from the midst of a bush. So he looked, and behold, the bush burned with fire, but the bush was not consumed.
>
> Then Moses said, "I will now turn aside and see this great sight, why the bush does not burn." So when the Lord saw that he turned aside to look, God called to him from the midst of the bush and said, "Moses, Moses!" And he said, "Here I am."
>
> ...And the Lord said, "I have surely seen the oppression of My people who are in Egypt, and have heard their cry because of their taskmasters, for I know their sorrows. So I have come down to deliver them out of the hand of the Egyptians, and to bring them up from that land to a good and large land, to a land flowing with milk and honey" (Ex. 3:2-4,7-8).

The dialogue between God and Moses continues into Exodus 3 and 4. As a matter of fact, for the remainder of his life, Moses heard God's voice and received His revelations.

God Spoke to a Barren Woman

Judges 13 records a most unusual series of events. The preincarnate Christ appeared to Manoah's wife, who had no children, and announced that she would become pregnant and bare a son. In answer to Manoah's prayer that the angel of the Lord would appear once more and teach them how to rear the child who was to be born, the Lord came to Manoah's wife a few days later as she sat alone in the field.

The Lord waited while the excited woman ran to fetch her husband and answered all their questions patiently.

Then He waited for them to build a fire on a nearby rock and offer up a goat and a cereal offering to God. Imagine the couple's astonishment as their supernatural Messenger suddenly ascended in the flames. (See Judg. 13:19-20.)

What is the outcome of the story? The child born to Manoah and his wife was Samson, the Old Testament "strong man" who helped deliver Israel out of the hand of the Philistines.

God Spoke to Samuel

In 1 Samuel 3, we find the beautiful story of the call of Samuel. I see little Samuel as a type of most contemporary evangelicals and charismatics; Samuel was ministering faithfully to the Lord, yet the Lord's voice had not yet been revealed to him.

Verse one deserves special attention, for it highlights the problem: "Then the boy Samuel ministered to the Lord before Eli. And the word of the Lord was *rare* in those days; there was no widespread revelation" (italics mine). God was speaking, but nobody was hearing. As in our day, God's voice was extended throughout all the earth, but humanity was not hearing that voice. It was as though mankind was on the wrong frequency, and nobody was trying to get tuned in. Consequently, the word of the Lord was rarely heard.

But, in little Samuel, God found someone who would listen. Even today, God will find a way to make His voice heard and understood by those who are ministering to Him out of a pure heart.

> And it came to pass at that time, while Eli was lying down in his place, and when his eyes had begun to grow so dim that he could not see, and before the lamp of God went out in the tabernacle of the Lord where the ark of God was, and while

Samuel was lying down to sleep, that the Lord called Samuel. And he answered, "Here I am!"

So he ran to Eli and said, "Here I am, for you called me." And he said, "I did not call; lie down again." And he went and lay down. And the Lord called yet again, "Samuel!" So Samuel arose and went to Eli, and said, "Here I am, for you called me." And he answered, "I did not call, my son; lie down again." (Now Samuel did not yet know the Lord, nor was the word of the Lord yet revealed to him.)

And the Lord called Samuel again the third time. Then he arose and went to Eli, and said, "Here I am, for you did call me." Then Eli perceived that the Lord had called the boy. Therefore Eli said to Samuel, "Go, lie down; and it shall be, if He calls you, that you must say, 'Speak, Lord, for Your servant hears.'" So Samuel went and lay down in his place.

Then the Lord came and stood and called as at other times, "Samuel! Samuel!" And Samuel answered, "Speak, for Your servant hears" (1 Sam. 3:2-10).

At this time in his life, Samuel was committed to the Lord, but he did not yet have that intimate, walking and talking relationship with God that he enjoyed later in life. Samuel knew the Lord in the way that the New Testament writers refer to as *ginosko*, but he did not yet enjoy the deeper, clearer, more thorough knowledge and appreciation of God which New Testament writers call *epiginosko*. He did not know the Lord with a full, inner knowledge. But as Samuel grew, spiritually as well as physically, he became intimately acquainted with God's voice. It wasn't long before all Israel knew that Samuel was established to be a prophet of the Lord. (See 1 Sam. 3:19-21.)

Please listen to me very carefully. Your real ministry begins when you start to discern the voice of the Lord in your spirit. Your real ministry is directed by the inner voice; real ministry begins as you walk, talk and dialogue with God. The problem with most of us is that, like Samuel, we don't realize that it is God's voice we are hearing. Just as Samuel assumed the voice was Eli's, we often think it's only another person speaking to us, or we assume that an inner voice is our own imagination, when all the time, it is God who is trying to get our attention.

God Spoke to Isaiah

Keep in mind that I'm not conducting a comprehensive study of God speaking to men and women in the Old Testament; I'm only laying groundwork and defining principles. Let's flip ahead to the Book of Isaiah. Once again the principle that real ministry is birthed out of hearing the voice of God is underscored. Isaiah declared:

I heard the voice of the Lord, saying:
"Whom shall I send,
And who will go for Us?"
Then I said, "Here am I! Send me."
And He said, "Go, and tell this people..." (Is. 6:8-9).

The secret to Isaiah's ministry was that he heard God's voice. God told him what to do, and he did it. Listen, my friend. Anything you hear God tell you to do, you can do with power, confidence, anointing and direction. Why? Because the word of the Lord has innate power to enable you to do what He has commanded.

God Spoke to Jeremiah

Let this sink deep down into your spirit: *You are important to God.* He created you for a purpose, and He longs to communicate that purpose to you and enable you to fulfill it. Consider God's words to Jeremiah:

> Then the word of the Lord came to me saying: "Before I formed you in the womb I knew you; before you were born I sanctified you; and I ordained you a prophet to the nations" (Jer. 1:4-5).

People may say, "That was only for Jeremiah. He was a special case." But that's not the way my Bible reads. Peter said: "...God shows no partiality. But in every nation whoever fears Him and works righteousness is accepted by Him" (Acts 10:34-35).

When Jeremiah questioned his own importance, God commanded:

> "Do not say, 'I am a youth,' for you shall go to all to whom I send you, and whatever I command you, you shall speak. Do not be afraid of their faces, for I am with you to deliver you," says the Lord (Jer. 1:7-8).

I believe that my friend James Robison is one of the greatest men of God living in the world today. Recently, six other men and I sat in a room and saw James cry like a baby as he shared his testimony.[1]

James, as you may have heard him testify, was an illegitimate child. Because his mother was unmarried and pregnant as a result of rape, she wanted an abortion, but her doctor said no. Because a God-fearing doctor refused to allow that unborn baby's life to be terminated, God was able to gift our nation with a mighty evangelist and prophet.

Your name may not be Isaiah, Jeremiah or James Robison, but you are important to God; moreover, He has a purpose for your life. I want to say it again, and I want you to hear it. The voice of the Lord gives direct, specific revelation. You can hear that voice.

In the Old Testament examples we have studied, God wasn't just sending out mystical signals or weird impressions. God didn't just "impress" Noah that he should build an ark; He told him what to do, how to do it and gave him specific instructions. God didn't just send out some sort of mystical "vibrations" to Moses that he was to deliver Israel out of Egyptian bondage; He gave Moses a definite, clear call.

Moses said, "Oh, that all the Lord's people were prophets and that the Lord would put His Spirit upon them!" (Num. 11:29). And God *has* ordained every New Testament believer to be a minister of the gospel—not necessarily one of the fivefold ministry gifts of apostle, prophet, evangelist, pastor or teacher (Eph. 4:11-12)—but a minister, nevertheless.

Not long ago, a man who has been in the ministry for many years approached me. Although his sincerity and concern for me were evident, I have to chuckle inside each time I think about it. "Larry," he warned, "you've got a bad problem at Church on the Rock."

"Really? What is it?" I asked.

His reply went something like this: "Well, every person in your church thinks that he or she is a minister. While you and your staff are ministering to people at the altars, your members think they may give words of encouragement or exhortation. They're going around preaching and praying for people!"

When I heard that, I was so proud of my people I felt like applauding. You see, we teach our people that every believer has an anointing—the anointing of the person of the Holy Spirit abiding within. Every believer has a ministry, but to fulfill that ministry, we must come to hear, recognize and obey the voice of the Spirit speaking to our spirits.

If that sounds good to you, read on. The Bible has much more to say regarding hearing ears.

Summing It Up

Take a moment to review what you have studied in chapter one about the hearing ear. God wants you to have "hearing ears." But you must develop your spiritual ears to the point that you know and understand God's voice when He speaks to your spirit.

Second, God spoke clearly and specifically to people in the Old Testament. Noah, Abraham, Moses, Samuel, Jeremiah, among others, received direct commands and promises from God, not vague impressions.

You may not be a Noah, a Moses or a Samuel, but God also has a special purpose for your life. To fulfill that purpose, you need to be able to hear, understand and obey God's voice. You need hearing ears.

Personal Growth Activity 1

1. Of the many thoughts presented in this first chapter, this one point made the deepest impression upon my heart:

_____

_____

_____

_____

_____

2. I believe that God still speaks to people.
   _____ Definitely
   _____ I'm not sure yet but I'm open to truth, even if it conflicts with my personal beliefs.

CHAPTER TWO

God Wants
To Speak to You

When my son, John Aaron, was just a few months old, before I left for work each morning I'd lean over his baby bed, take his tiny hand in mine and say, "Hey, John Aaron, this is Dad. It's time for me to go out and get in the car and drive down to the church. We're going to reach people for Jesus today." As I talked, John would coo and smile, wave his little arms and blow bubbles. Why? Because he was hearing a voice that was familiar to him. He knew that his daddy was there.

Did John understand what it meant to start the car and drive down the street? Could he comprehend what I was telling him? No. But as he continued to mature and develop, he began to understand all those things. Now that he's a teenager, he wants to arm wrestle and work out with me, and he can understand what I'm saying to him—usually.

In a typical church congregation, we can look around us and see human beings in all stages of physical maturity—infants, children, young adults, the elderly, teenagers, the middle-aged. But we all go through various spiritual stages, too. God wants to bring us through infancy, childhood and adolescence, all the way to completeness and maturity in our relationships with Him. God longs for His sons and daughters to mature in our hearing and spiritual understanding to the point where we can hear His words and use those words to bring glory to Him and to bless others. Perhaps I should share an example to illustrate how this works.

John Wimber's name and ministry have become familiar to many believers. Some time ago, John, the director of Vineyard Ministries, was flying on a 747, minding his own business and meditating on the things of God, when he happened to glance at a man sitting nearby. To his amazement, John's spiritual eyes saw a woman's name written across the man's forehead.

Sensing what God was about to ask him to do, John protested silently, "Lord, I just want to read my Bible and pray."

But the Lord said, "Ask the man if that woman's name means anything to him."

So John spoke to the man (who happened to be seated beside his wife) and inquired, "Does such and such a name mean anything to you?"

It turned out that the man was having an affair with a woman of that name. He and John went up in the top of the 747, and the man repented and gave his heart to the Lord. Then the man's wife joined them, and she, too, turned her life over to God.[1]

For your sake, others' sake and His own sake, God wants to mature you spiritually and get you to the place where you can hear His Spirit speak clearly.

You may be thinking, OK, I know that God spoke to people in the Old Testament. But is there any precedent for this in New Testament times?

I'm going to make a very important point right here,

so please pay close attention. If God spoke to people in the Old Testament under the old covenant, common sense tells us that believers under the new covenant should enjoy at least equal privileges. As a matter of fact, we should enjoy even better privileges. According to the writer of Hebrews, because of Jesus believers under the new covenant enjoy: "a better hope" (Heb. 7:19); "a better covenant" (7:22); "better promises" (8:6); "better sacrifices" (9:23); "a better and an enduring possession" for ourselves in heaven (10:34); and "a better resurrection" (11:35).

The book of Hebrews was written to say one thing, primarily: better, better, better, better! If God spoke to individuals under the old covenant, He will also speak to believers under the new covenant. And the way He chooses to speak will be even better.

The New Testament

As we turn through the pages of the New Testament, an unmistakable fact emerges: God still spoke to individuals during New Testament times. From Matthew to Revelation, people with hearing ears were receiving God's words.

Jesus Spoke to His Disciples

At the beginning of His earthly ministry, Jesus chose twelve disciples. Why? Mark says simply, "He appointed twelve that they might be with Him..." (Mark 3:14). Somehow these twelve friends, imperfect and earthly as they turned out to be, were an encouragement and a help to Jesus. Do you know what that says to me? It says that God longs for our fellowship and friendship. He enjoys our communion. He yearns for the intimate dialogue of our prayers.

Jesus communicated freely with His disciples. He taught them, explained God's plans and purposes to them and corrected them. He spoke freely and clearly to the disciples. He didn't communicate through mental "vibrations" or intangible impressions. (See Mark 1:35-38; Matt. 24:3-8, for example.)

In John 10, we see what Jesus taught His disciples about hearing and knowing His voice:

> ..And the sheep hear his [the shepherd's] voice; and he calls his own sheep by name and leads them out. And when he brings out his own sheep, he goes before them; and the sheep follow him, for they know his voice. Yet they will by no means follow a stranger, but will flee from him, for they do not know the voice of strangers....
>
> I am the good shepherd; and I know My sheep, and am known by My own....
>
> And other sheep I have which are not of this fold; them also I must bring, and they will hear My voice; and there will be one flock and one shepherd....
>
> My sheep hear My voice, and I know them, and they follow Me (vv. 3-5,14,16,27).

According to the Word of God, Christ's disciples are to know, hear and obey His voice.

Jesus Promised to Send the Holy Spirit

Just before His ascension, Jesus assembled His disciples and commanded them not to depart from Jerusalem but to wait for the promised Holy Spirit. He said:

> John truly baptized with water, but you shall be baptized with the Holy Spirit not many days from now....

28

But you shall receive power when the Holy
Spirit has come upon you; and you shall be
witnesses to Me in Jerusalem, and in all Judea and
Samaria, and to the end of the earth (Acts 1:5,8).

After New Testament believers were filled with the
promised Holy Spirit, they became powerful witnesses
for Christ.

They weren't left to flounder along on their own. Acts
and the Epistles are filled with illustrations of people
receiving clear-cut directions and instructions from the
Spirit of God.

God Spoke to Philip

Philip, a deacon whom God called to do the work of
evangelism in Samaria, was led by a definite directive of
the Holy Spirit to speak to an Ethiopian eunuch:

Then the Spirit said to Philip, "Go near and overtake this chariot." So Philip ran to him, and heard
him reading the prophet Isaiah, and said, "Do you
understand what you are reading?" And he said,
"How can I, unless someone guides me?" And he
asked Philip to come up and sit with him....
Then Philip opened his mouth, and...preached
Jesus to him (Acts 8:29-31,35).

How clearly the Spirit spoke to Philip! It wasn't some
nebulous impression. Maybe there were ten chariots out
there in the desert. But the Spirit said, "Overtake *this*
chariot."

In Acts 21:8-9, Luke informs us that Philip had four
maiden daughters who had the gift of prophecy. Not only
did Philip hear from God—his godly daughters were also
intimately acquainted with the voice of the Spirit and
spoke forth inspired words of comfort, exhortation and

edification (See 1 Cor. 14:3.)

God Spoke to Ananias

After the story of Philip and the eunuch, in the very next chapter of Acts, the Lord appears to a Damascan disciple named Ananias. Notice what clear, specific directives this man received from the Lord. Notice also that the Lord carried on a conversation with Ananias; it was a dialogue, not a monologue:

> So the Lord said to him, "Arise and go to the street called Straight, and inquire at the house of Judas for one called Saul of Tarsus, for behold, he is praying.
>
> And in a vision he has seen a man named Ananias coming in and putting his hand on him, so that he might receive his sight."
>
> Then Ananias answered, "Lord, I have heard from many about this man, how much harm he has done to Your saints in Jerusalem. And here he has authority from the chief priests to bind all who call on Your name."
>
> But the Lord said to him, "Go, for he is a chosen vessel of Mine to bear My name before Gentiles, kings, and the children of Israel. For I will show him how many things he must suffer for My name's sake" (Acts 9:11-16).

God Spoke to Cornelius

We have seen that God spoke to Philip, a deacon, and to Ananias, a disciple. Next, in Acts 10, God sent an angel to speak in a vision with a devout man named Cornelius, a centurion in what was known as the Italian Regiment:

> About the ninth hour of the day he [Cornelius] saw clearly in a vision an angel of God coming in and

30

saying to him, "Cornelius!"

And when he observed him, he was afraid, and said, "What is it, lord?" So he said to him, "Your prayers and your alms have come up for a memorial before God.

Now send men to Joppa, and send for Simon whose surname is Peter. He is lodging with Simon, a tanner, whose house is by the sea. He will tell you what you must do" (Acts 10:3-6).

God Spoke to Peter

The very next day, as two servants sent by Cornelius drew near the city of Joppa, God prepared the apostle Peter's heart for their visit by showing him a vision of all kinds of animals, beasts and birds and then by teaching him an important lesson:

And a voice came to him, "Rise, Peter; kill and eat."

But Peter said, "Not so, Lord! For I have never eaten anything common or unclean."

And a voice spoke to him again the second time, "What God has cleansed you must not call common."

This was done three times. And the object was taken up into heaven again (Acts 10:13-16).

While Peter thought about the vision, the Spirit of God spoke to him and gave him specific instructions: "Behold, three men are seeking you. Arise therefore, go down and go with them, doubting nothing; for I have sent them" (Acts 10:19-20).

God Spoke to the Apostle Paul

In Acts 16, Luke, the physician who accompanied the apostle Paul and his evangelistic party on a missionary journey, recorded:

> Now when they had gone through Phrygia and the
> region of Galatia, they were forbidden by the Holy
> Spirit to preach the word in Asia. After they had
> come to Mysia, they tried to go into Bithynia, but
> the Spirit did not permit them (vv. 6-7).

Luke did not tell us how the Spirit communicated these messages to Paul and his companions. But he did tell us that one night a man of Macedonia stood before Paul in a vision and pleaded with him to come to Macedonia and help them. Luke said: "Now after he had seen the vision, immediately we sought to go to Macedonia, concluding that the Lord had called us to preach the gospel to them" (Acts 16:10).

What have we learned from this handful of New Testament examples? For one thing, we have seen that God did not speak only with the twelve apostles; He also spoke with ordinary people, such as deacons, disciples and centurions. We have also seen that God is perfectly capable of delivering clear, specific, understandable messages and that people are able to receive and comprehend His words.

I realize some will argue that the reason the Spirit of God spoke directly to individuals during New Testament times was that the Bible was not yet completed. The Bible was not yet a closed canon.

Allow me to address that argument. I don't want anyone to get the idea that I am trying to add words to the Word of God, for we are not to add or subtract anything from the Bible.

But the Bible is God's Word written to bring us to the person of Jesus. The Word of God rightly understood reveals that He lives on the inside of believers. By teaching you how to hear and obey His voice, I am not adding anything to the Bible. Instead, I am implementing the *purpose* of the Bible.

Believers have walked in the natural realm so long that they are afraid of the supernatural. We've been so pragmatic, living by religious principles, that we have forgotten that the *principles* of the Bible were put there to lead us to a *person*. That's exactly what Jesus meant when He said to the Pharisees: "You search the Scriptures, for in them you think you have eternal life; and these are they which testify of *Me*" (John 5:39, italics mine).

God speaks to us through His Word. Certainly. Most assuredly. But He also communicates with the inner man through the voice of His Holy Spirit. He still communicates specifically and understandably to the believer who has an ear to hear.

God Wants to Speak to You

Jesus specifically commanded His disciples to wait in Jerusalem until they were endued with power from on high. Why was it so important that the followers of Jesus be filled with the Holy Spirit? One reason was that the Spirit would empower and enable them to be witnesses. But in John 16, Jesus explained still more about the work of the Spirit.

> Nevertheless I tell you the truth. It is to your advantage that I go away; for if I do not go away, the Helper will not come to you; but if I depart, I will send Him to you....
>
> I still have many things to say to you, but you cannot bear them now. However, when He, the Spirit of truth, has come, He will guide you into

33

all truth; for He will not speak on His own authority, but whatever He hears He will speak; and He will tell you things to come. He will glorify Me, for He will take of what is Mine and declare it to you. All things that the Father has are Mine. Therefore, I said that He will take of Mine and declare it to you (vv. 7,12-15).

Receive the Spirit's Revelation

Jesus promised that the Holy Spirit would live in believers, receive what Jesus speaks to Him and tell us what He says. The Holy Spirit is continually receiving information from Jesus concerning things to come in your life and in the lives of those around you. The Bible says that the Holy Spirit receives messages from Jesus and that He is within us in order to reveal Christ's words and will to us. That is how New Testament Christianity functions.

When you are born again, Someone who is wise and good, righteous and holy, sanctifying and strengthening comes into your heart. As you listen to His voice and obey Him and learn to walk and talk with Him, His life and presence within you produce righteousness, peace and joy, and you will not fulfill the lusts of the flesh. You will not be governed by external rules; instead, you will walk according to His Word and by inner revelation from a person who lives inside you.

That's what I mean by New Testament Christianity. The Old Testament principle was legalism, struggling to attain acceptance by God. But the New Testament believer lives by hearing, obeying and being empowered by a living person on the inside, the Holy Spirit.

Fellowship With the Spirit of God

In Philippians 2:1-2, Paul wrote:

> Therefore if there is any consolation in Christ, if any comfort of love, if any *fellowship of the Spirit*, if any affection and mercy, fulfill my job by being like-minded, having the same love, being of one accord, of one mind (italics mine).

The word "fellowship" (*koinonia*) implies a give-and-take relationship. Jesus said: "If I do not go away, the Comforter (Counselor, Helper, Advocate, Intercessor, Strengthener, Standby) will not come to you—into close fellowship with you. But if I go away, I will send Him to you—to be in close fellowship with you" (John 16:7, Amplified).

This same idea of fellowship and spiritual communion is illustrated in Revelation 3:20. Jesus said: "Behold, I stand at the door and knock. If anyone hears My voice and opens the door, I will come in to him and dine with him, and he with Me." The root word in the Greek for "dine" (or "sup" as the King James Version translates it) is the same as that for *koinonia*. The idea here is of two people sitting down to eat together, getting to know each other, supping from each other's spirits, communing and conversing intimately with each other.

And consider the words of Paul's apostolic benediction in 2 Corinthians 13:14: "The grace of the Lord Jesus Christ, and the love of God, and the communion of the Holy Spirit be with you all." The word "communion" is actually the Greek word *koinonia*. W.E. Vine, in his *Expository Dictionary of Old and New Testament Words*, defines *koinonia* as it is used here as "a having in common, partnership, fellowship recognized and enjoyed, a participation in what is derived from the Holy Spirit."

35

As we learn to hear and obey the voice of the Spirit of God within our spirits, we will come to cherish His wisdom and revelation. We will covet His intimate friendship. We will enjoy the communion—the fellowship—of the Spirit.

Dr. Wayne Inzer, his wife, Mickey, and their two teenage daughters are members of our church. Since 1986, Wayne and Mickey have led a prayer meeting from 5 to 6 *a.m.*, Monday through Thursday, in a place of business near their home.

Mickey explains, "I know that God wants me to minister to people, so as I'm praying every morning, I ask, 'God, what is Your word for the person You will bring across my path today?' Then I wait to receive a word, a verse of Scripture or some definite impression upon my spirit. All through the day I seek to walk in communion and fellowship with the Holy Spirit. When that little "buzzer" goes off inside, signaling that this is the person I'm to speak to, I already know what I'm supposed to say. I just wait for the Holy Spirit to tell me how and when to say it."

Mickey continues, "I talk to God as if I'm talking to somebody, not some thing. I speak to Him, and then I give Him a chance to answer. I expect to hear from God. I seek to walk in fellowship with the Holy Spirit, and I expect Him to speak and guide me."

Wayne and Mickey have developed the practice of praying with their daughters regarding any major decision in their household. First, their family prays together in the Spirit. After that, they listen, fully expecting God to speak to each of them.

Wayne is a gynecologist. After leading the early-morning prayer meetings, he puts to good use the time it takes to drive to his office by meditating on Scripture and communing with the Holy Spirit.

One morning Wayne was driving along, meditating on the story of Philip and the Ethiopian eunuch, found in the book of Acts. Imagine what it would be like to be led by the Spirit as Philip was, he mused. Wouldn't it be wonderful to have the privilege of bringing the Word of the Lord to someone as hungry for God as that Ethiopian man?

Shortly after that prayer, another physician called Wayne and asked him to serve as a consultant on a case—a patient in a psychiatric ward. Although the woman had been admitted because of severe psychological problems, she also had gynecological problems that needed attention.

Later that day, as he paused at the nurses' station outside the psychiatric ward to read the patient's medical records, his heart ached. Fact after fact pointed out sorrow and personal tragedy endured by this woman. Lord, he sighed prayerfully, if anybody ever needed You, this woman does.

As he entered the patient's room, he noticed on her bedside table a tract titled *You Can Know God*. Wayne introduced himself, conducted the examination requested by his colleague and made the necessary notes. But, in his heart, he knew that he was also in that room at the invitation of the Great Physician.

Sensing in his spirit that God was opening a door for him to share Jesus, Wayne picked up the tract he had noticed earlier and asked, "Do you know how to find God?"

He could hardly believe the woman's answer, for her reply was like an echo of the Ethiopian's answer to Philip's question. "How can I," the woman said hopelessly, "if I don't have anybody to tell me?"

Wayne stepped boldly through the door of opportunity the Holy Spirit opened to him and led the desperate woman to God.

God spoke to people in the Old Testament. He communicated with people in the New Testament. And He is still speaking to people like John Wimber and Wayne Inzer—people who have hearing ears.

By the way—when was the last time *you* heard His voice?

Summing It Up

New Testament believers, like people in the Old Testament, have a definite place in God's plan and are called to carry out certain ministries. But if we are to fulfill God's purposes for our lives, we must hear, recognize and obey the voice of the Lord just as God's people did in the Old Testament.

God communicated with people in the New Testament. Jesus spoke directly to His disciples, not through vague impressions. Jesus called Himself the shepherd, and He said that His sheep, His followers, should know, hear and obey His voice. Jesus also promised to send the Holy Spirit to lead and empower believers and impart His truth to them.

God wants to speak to all of His followers, including you. The Holy Spirit within you receives messages from Jesus in order to reveal Christ's words and will to you. As you learn to hear His voice speaking within your spirit and obey His commands, His life and presence within you will produce righteousness, peace and joy. You will walk by both the Word of God and by inner revelation from the Holy Spirit who lives inside you.

God Wants to Speak to You

Personal Growth Activity 2

1. My "spiritual ears" have heard God speaking to me:

    ____ Frequently   ____ Rarely
    ____ Sometimes   ____ Never

2. The last time I heard God speaking to me, He said:

    _____
    _____
    _____
    _____
    _____
    _____

3. My spiritual ears are developed to the place that:

    ____ I hear clear, specific words from God in my spirit.
    ____ I "muddle my way through" on vague impressions.
    ____ I rarely, if ever, have heard God speaking to me; when I want to know what God is saying, I rely on someone else who seems to hear from God.

4. I believe that God wants to speak to me and that I can develop "hearing ears."

    ____ Definitely
    ____ I'm still not convinced, but I'm willing to continue studying the subject.

SECTION TWO

Removing Hindrances to Hearing

CHAPTER THREE

Three Big Ones

D o you mean to tell me that you hear God speaking to you?" questioned a man after hearing me preach. The expression on his face was a mixture of amazement, sarcasm and skepticism. Not batting an eye, I bounced the "ball" back in his court: "Do you mean to tell me that God *doesn't* speak to you?" Then I explained that salvation should lead to a *relationship* with Jesus.

Remember, Jesus said, "My sheep hear My voice" (John 10:27). God wants our spiritual ears to be open so we can hear the voice of the Spirit of God.

Although you may try to keep your spiritual ears open, you will struggle with one or more of five basic hindrances to hearing God's voice. In this chapter and in the next, we will examine these hindrances.

Unbelief

The first basic hindrance to hearing God is *unbelief*. In section one, I emphasized that God wants to speak to you and that you can hear God. We saw that, in Old Testament times, God spoke to people such as Moses and Abraham, to prophets such as Jeremiah and Isaiah, pointing to the time when Jesus Christ, the Jewish Messiah and the Savior of the world, would come. We saw that God also communicated with individuals in the New Testament.

John spoke of Christ as the "Word" of God:

> In the beginning was the Word, and the Word was with God, and the Word was God....
> And the Word became flesh and dwelt among us, and we beheld His glory... (John 1:1,14).

The Word was made flesh—the Word dwelt among us. Exactly what does a word do? A word is a communicator. If I speak a word to you, that is communication. Jesus, the manifested Word of God, spoke to His disciples and to the people around Him, communicating His Father's plan and purposes.

During His earthly ministry, Jesus sometimes spoke to hundreds, even thousands, of people at once. But hindered by His physical flesh, Jesus could not be in more than one place at once or speak to more than a few thousand people at one time. That was one of the reasons He said: "Nevertheless I tell you the truth. It is to your advantage that I go away; for if I do not go away, the Helper will not come to you; but if I depart, I will send Him to you" (John 16:7).

When Jesus said, "It's better for you that I go away, because if I don't go away, I can't send the Holy Spirit to you," I think the disciples must have scratched their heads and wondered why it would really be better for them if He went away. After all, He walked by their sides and talked with them. They heard His teachings and saw His miracles. How could it possibly be better if He went away?

The disciples did not realize that through the presence

of the Holy Spirit, Jesus would be able to speak not with just one man or woman or a few thousand people at one time; He would be able to reveal Himself to all believers. In addition, He would no longer simply be *with* a few beloved followers; through the person of the Holy Spirit, He would be *in* all believers.

Jesus had explained this to the disciples, but they had not grasped His meaning:

> I will pray the Father, and He will give you another Helper, that He may abide with you forever, even the Spirit of truth, whom the world cannot receive, because it neither sees Him nor knows Him; but you know Him, for He dwells *with* you and will be *in* you (John 14:16,17, italics mine).

As Paul put it later, "...Christ *in* you, the hope of glory" (Col. 1:27, italics mine). If you are a Christian, you have Jesus Christ living within you. I'm not talking about a Christ "type" or "influence." I don't mean a Christ "ideology" or "philosophy." I'm talking about Jesus: the God-man who preached and performed miracles along the shores of the Sea of Galilee 2,000 years ago. I'm referring to Jesus, the resurrected, living Son of God who is the same yesterday, today and forever (Heb. 13:8).

Stop and think about something with me. During His earthly ministry when the Son of God was clothed in the flesh and blood of man, He walked in the anointing and power of the Spirit. He healed the sick, the lame and the maimed; opened blind eyes and deaf ears; cast out devils and raised the dead.

But after Christ was crucified and resurrected, things changed. He still talked, ate and walked with His disciples. As a matter of fact, in His resurrected state, He could walk right through walls or locked doors. He could

45

suddenly appear or disappear. Peter probably exclaimed: "Lord, we need to show You off! Let's all go down to Jerusalem Hospital, and You can heal every sick person in the place. Then we can walk down the street to the morgue, and You can raise all the dead. Then let's head for the insane asylum and let You clear it out!"

But in those days after Christ's resurrection and before His ascension, we don't have a single record where He laid His hands on another sick person and healed them or cast out another devil. Instead, He told His followers that *they* were to preach the gospel, cast out the demons, heal the sick and raise the dead. (See Mark 16:17-18.)

Why did Jesus give such a command? Why didn't He carry on His ministry as He had done before? Because they, His church, were His new body. (See 1 Cor. 12:27.) They were now His hands, His feet, His eyes and His voice.

As believers, you and I are a part of Christ's body on this earth today. The Spirit of Christ has taken up residence in our bodies, which He calls His temples (1 Cor. 6:19), and He wants to walk with us, talk with us and work signs and wonders through us. (See 1 Cor. 12.)

Now some people will back up from this truth and caution, "Be careful now. It's dangerous to tell people that they can hear God speak to them or that the gifts and power of the Holy Spirit can operate through them." Listen, anything that's worth something has the potential to be dangerous in one way or another. But don't misunderstand. I'm not trying to cause confusion or to trouble others. I'm trying to help transfer believers into New Testament Christianity, into the wonderful realm where they walk and talk with God.

Have you ever believed something with your head but not with your heart? This is the very plight in which some

Christians find themselves when they read Christ's words, "My sheep hear My voice" (John 10:27). "That's a great verse," they mumble to themselves. "It's got to be true because it's written in the Bible. But does God really want to speak to *me*?"

Does God want to speak to you? That's the issue you must resolve. If you are ever to hear from God, you must come to the point where you believe in your own heart that God does indeed want to speak to you. Why? Because everything in the kingdom of God functions by faith. Take a moment to scan the following Scripture verses, and you'll understand what I mean.

First of all, what is faith? According to the Amplified Bible:

> Faith is the assurance (the confirmation, the title-deed) of the things [we] hope for, being the proof of things [we] do not see and the conviction of their reality—faith perceiving as real fact what is not revealed to the senses (Heb. 11:1).

Think about faith and the vital role it plays in life:

We are saved through faith. "For by grace you have been saved through faith, and that not of yourselves; it is the gift of God..." (Eph. 2:8).

We are sanctified by faith. At Paul's conversion, Jesus told him that He was sending him to the Gentiles so that "they may receive forgiveness of sins and an inheritance among those who are sanctified by faith in Me" (Acts 26:18).

We are justified by faith. In his letter to the believers at Rome, Paul declared: "Therefore, having been justified by faith, we have peace with God through our Lord Jesus Christ" (Rom. 5:1).

We walk and live by faith. "For we walk by faith, not

by sight" (2 Cor. 5:7; see also Gal. 2:20; 3:11).

We use the shield of faith "with which you will be able to quench all the fiery darts of the wicked one" (Eph. 6:16).

Our righteousness comes from God by faith. Paul told the Philippians that he did not want to be found in his own righteousness, which was from the law. Rather, he desired the righteousness "which is through faith in Christ, the righteousness which is from God by faith" (Phil. 3:9).

We are "*rooted and built up in Him [Jesus] and established in the faith*" (Col. 2:7).

Faith transforms the impossible to the possible. Jesus said: "If you have faith as a mustard seed, you will say to this mountain, 'Move from here to there,' and it will move; and nothing will be impossible for you" (Matt. 17:20).

Healing comes through faith. When the lame man at the Beautiful Gate of the temple was healed, Peter declared: "And His name, through faith in His name, has made this man strong, whom you see and know. Yes, the faith which comes through Him has given him this perfect soundness in the presence of you all" (Acts 3:16).

The prayer of faith saves the sick (James 5:15).

John informs us that *our faith is the victory that conquers and overcomes the world* (1 John 5:4).

According to Romans 14:23, *"whatever is not of faith is sin."*

After this brief survey of the Scriptures regarding faith, it is not hard to comprehend why the author of Hebrews emphatically declared: "Without faith, it is impossible to please Him [God]" (Heb. 11:6). But the writer does not stop there; he goes on to state: "...he who comes to God must believe that He is, and that He is a rewarder of those who diligently seek Him."

It takes faith to believe that there is a God who hears and answer your prayers, a God who also wants to speak to *you*.

Now it's time to go on to maturity and become walking, talking sons and daughters of God who know, hear and obey His voice. It's time to realize that Someone is living inside us and that there's nothing wrong with His mouth or ears. He can speak, and He listens when we talk to Him. We must break through the obstacle of unbelief and refuse to allow it to continue to hinder the line of communication between God and us.

An Undeveloped Spirit

Humans are triune beings. Paul stated this very clearly to the Thessalonian believers when he said: "Now may the God of peace Himself sanctify you completely; and may your whole *spirit, soul, and body* be preserved blameless at the coming of our Lord Jesus Christ" (1 Thess. 5:23, italics mine).

Notice the order in which Paul puts these three aspects of mankind. He does not say: body, soul (mind, will and emotions) and spirit, but spirit, soul and body.

Often we human beings place the most importance upon our bodies, forgetting that some day our physical bodies will cease functioning. Even after death, our spirits will live on—forever. We carefully feed, clothe, exercise and pamper our physical flesh but think nothing of starving and neglecting our spirits.

Men and women are spirit beings, made in the likeness of God, who is a Spirit. (See Gen. 1:26-27; John 4:24.) You see, humans *live* in physical bodies, *have* souls and *are* spirits. They have an inward spirit being that will live forever, and they have an outward physical being.

(See 2 Cor. 4:16.) The physical being is not the real person; it is only the temporary, clay house in which the inward spirit being lives.

For example, the garments hanging in your closet are not the real you. They are only the clothing your body wears. Just so, your physical body is not the real you. It is only the clothing your inward spirit being wears. Some day, if the Lord tarries, your physical body will die, be buried and crumble to dust. But your spirit being will live forever.

Some believers develop their minds and/or their personalities. They accumulate degree after degree or attend one relational seminar after another. Others work hard to develop their bodies. They exercise and work out with weights. They jog and take special care to eat only the right foods. These things are good. But how many believers are working just as diligently in order to develop their spirits?

Why should our spirits be developed? The Scriptures clearly teach that if we want to be able to hear God and receive His guidance, we must develop our spirits, for it is through our spirits that God leads us. According to Romans 8:14,16, "For as many as are led by the Spirit of God, these are the sons of God....The Spirit Himself bears witness with our *spirit* that we are children of God" (italics mine).

If we expect to be led by the Spirit of God, we must develop the ability to hear. We must develop our spirits. How do we do this?

I will discuss this subject at length in later chapters, but here I will briefly list some of the steps.

Reading and meditating on the Word of God develops our spirits, but this is not enough. We must obey the Word if we want strong spiritual muscles. Prayer also develops our spirits. As we worship and commune with God, spending time in His presence, His mighty Holy Spirit reinforces our inner person. Further, as we learn to pray in the Spirit and listen for God's word to us, our spirits are built up. As we make these biblical practices a way of life, we will grow mighty in spirit.

Some people may be thinking, Sure, Larry, that's easy for you to say. You're a preacher, and preachers are paid to read the Bible, pray and spend time with God. But after a hard day's work, I don't feel like reading the Bible or praying. I just need somewhere to crash!

May I let you in on a little secret? Preachers sometimes need to "crash," too. A well-known pastor friend of mine was asked by a group of young ministers what he did after preaching five times on Sunday. His unexpected answer brought the house down. In pious tones he droned, "I go home, put on my robe, sit down in front of the television...and watch something *violent!*"

I can relate to that. I had a television put in my study at home for much the same reason. But not long ago, the Spirit of God asked me to give Him more time in the Word and in prayer. For me, that meant taking the television out of my study.

Let's get real. After being out in the grind of the world all day, our spirits aren't going to be edified by "Miami Vice" or similar programs. If we want strong spirits, we must take the time to develop them.

A Spirit of Deafness

A third hindrance to hearing God's voice is spiritual deafness. This deafness comes primarily through the bondage of a spirit of deafness that blocks people's spiritual hearing. But how is a spirit of deafness enabled to put an individual in such bondage?

Most of us have been hurt at least once in our lives. The Word of God teaches that, as Christians, you and I are to forgive anyone who has hurt us (even if that person was ourselves), bring those wounds and wrongs to the Lord, allow Him to heal our hurts and then release it all to God. If we do not follow those steps, if we decide to walk in unforgiveness, we open up ourselves to what the Bible calls "tormentors" or "torturers."

Matthew 18:23-35 records a parable on forgiveness that Jesus taught His disciples. In the story, a king freely forgives his servant an enormous debt of 10,000 talents, knowing there is no way the man can ever repay such a sum. But the servant, to whom the king has shown such great mercy, refuses to be merciful and cancel the debt of a poor man who owes the servant a small amount of money. Instead, he grabs the man by the throat, demands that he pay all and, when the man can't, has him thrown into prison. When the king hears about his servant's hardheartedness and lack of forgiveness, he is furious and exclaims: "You wicked servant! I forgave you all that debt because you begged me. Should you not also have had compassion on your fellow servant, just as I had pity on you?" (vv. 32-33).

In conclusion, Jesus said: "And his master was angry, and delivered him to the *torturers* until he should pay all that was due to him. So My heavenly Father also will do to you if each of you, from his heart, does not forgive his brother his trespasses" (vv. 34-35, italics mine).

When we choose not to forgive others freely as God has forgiven us, we open ourselves up to tormentors— torturing thoughts, painful memories and oppressing spirits of darkness. As a result of our self-inflicted wounds and the works of evil spirits, our inner selves are damaged and slowly destroyed. The heart of our spirit-man grows

52

hard. Our spiritual ears gradually become insensitive or deaf to the voice of God.

Paul issued a stern warning along this line to the Ephesians:

> When angry, do not sin; do not ever let your wrath—your exasperation, your fury or indignation—last until the sun goes down. *Leave no [such] room or foothold for the devil*—give no opportunity to him (Eph. 4:26-27, Amplified, italics mine).

When we do not repent and allow God to cleanse our hearts, emotions such as anger, unforgiveness and jealousy give Satan a foothold in our lives and open the door to oppression and demonic attack. This is how many of God's people come to be oppressed by a spirit of spiritual deafness. They refuse to forgive. They reject the voice of the Holy Spirit as He convicts them of their sin and pleads with them to forgive and release those who have wronged them. Then when these believers want to hear God, they can't seem to break through. They pray. They wait. They strain and do everything they can think of, but their deaf ears do not hear His still, small voice.

How do we turn this process around? How can the spirit of deafness be rebuked and forced to release us from its oppressive bondage? We must first go to the root of the problem. We must get the bitterness, resentment and unforgiveness out of our spirits. We must forgive others for the hurts they have caused us (or forgive ourselves for the pain we have brought upon ourselves), just as God has forgiven us. We must allow the blood of Jesus to cleanse us from all sin; then we must release the past and let it go. As we begin walking in love and obedience to God's Word, we will have hearing ears that recognize and receive the word of the Lord as it comes to us.

At one point in my life I had a hard time forgiving my father for the grief he had caused my mom, my sister and me. His alcoholism contributed to an unstable home life for all of us. But a year or so after Jesus came into my heart and forgave me for all the hurts I had caused Him, I was finally able to pray, "God, I give my dad to You. I forgive him."

Do you know what I discovered after that? Bitterness and unforgiveness kill, but love heals. My attitude changed toward my dad, and intercession for him began to flow unobstructed from the bottom of my heart. You guessed it. It wasn't long until my dad pulled his car over to the side of the road and prayed, "God, if You can do anything with an old drunk like me, I'm Yours."

It's been over eighteen years since my dad prayed that prayer, and he's never had another drink. He's also become my best friend. But you'll never convince me that any of that would have happened if I had refused to forgive my father.

Do you want hearing ears? If so, you'll have to get past the hindrances of unbelief, an undeveloped spirit and a spirit of deafness released through your unwillingness to forgive.

After you make it past those obstacles to hearing, you'll be forced to confront two more hindrances to developing hearing ears: a calloused conscience and neglect. What do you say? Shall we go after them?

Summing It Up

In chapter three, we studied three basic hindrances to hearing God. Let's take a moment to summarize the most important points and set them in our minds.

1. *Unbelief.* It's time for us Christians to realize that Someone is living inside us and that there's nothing wrong with His ears or mouth. He listens when we talk to Him, and He wants to speak to us. But first, we must break through the obstacle of unbelief, refusing to allow it to continue to hinder the line of communication between God and us.

2. *An undeveloped spirit.* Humans are triune beings: spirit, soul and body. In order to be led by the Spirit of God, we must develop our spirits by reading and obeying God's Word and by prayer.

3. *A spirit of deafness.* When we choose not to forgive, we give Satan a foothold in our lives and open ourselves up to attack or oppression from evil spirits. One such spirit is a spirit of deafness that makes our spiritual ears insensitive to the Spirit of God. We must forgive those who have wronged us, release the past and walk in love and forgiveness.

If we want hearing ears, we must fight to overcome the obstacles of unbelief, an undeveloped spirit and a spirit of deafness. Only then can we hear the voice of the Spirit.

Personal Growth Activity 3

1. On a scale of 1 (greatest) to 3 (least), rank these hindrances as they have prevented you from hearing God:

    _____ Unbelief
    _____ An undeveloped spirit
    _____ A spirit of deafness

2. On the lines below, list at least three practical steps you plan to take in order to remove your number one hindrance to hearing God.

    _____
    _____
    _____

CHAPTER FOUR

More Hindrances

My mind wouldn't believe my ears. Surely I had misunderstood. But no, I had heard right. One of our pastors had spent tireless hours in prayer and counseling trying to help a man overcome his drinking problem. Now the guy was standing in front of me, repeating his ludicrous assertion: "Yep, God told me just to take the night off and go get drunk!"

If the whole situation hadn't been so pathetic, I'd have been tempted to laugh right out loud. This man had probably heard a voice all right, but it wasn't God's. How had he wandered so far off track?

A Calloused Conscience

We have already studied that humans are triune beings—spirit, soul (mind, will and emotions) and body. But perhaps you are not aware that every normal human being is continually receiving signals from his or her spirit, soul and body

Our bodies communicate with us through feelings. For example, our bodies send us messages by means of headaches, stomach aches, hunger, weakness and so forth, to let us know that something is wrong with us physically.

Our souls communicate with us through thinking or reasoning. If we are not careful, we can allow our thought lives to dominate us through worry, fear, hatred, lust, desires for pleasure or for revenge. We can even rationalize away our responsibilities or feelings of guilt.

If our bodies communicate with us through feelings, and our souls communicate with us through thinking or reasoning, how do our spirits communicate with us?

Your spirit communicates with you by means of your conscience. You know its familiar voice: "Don't do that." "You really should do so-and-so." "If you say that, you'll be sorry." "Don't make a decision yet. You don't know if this is really God's will." You know that voice, don't you.

You do not have to know or serve God to have a conscience. Both nonbelievers and believers hear the little, inner voices of their own human spirits speaking to them. But human consciences can lead people astray. Only when the conscience is reinforced by the Word of God and the voice of the indwelling Holy Spirit, is the Christian's conscience a safe, sure guide.

We know that Paul had learned to listen to the voice of his obedient, Spirit-sensitive conscience, for he declared: "I tell the truth in Christ, I am not lying, *my conscience also bearing me witness in the Holy Spirit...*" (Rom. 9:1, italics mine). Like Paul, we must listen to our consciences bearing witness to the message the Spirit of God has communicated to our spirits.

However, if we have allowed our consciences to be seared by sin and willful disobedience, if we have not received God's forgiveness and cleansing, our consciences will not be reliable. Paul made this clear in his letter to Timothy. The aged apostle warned:

> The (Holy) Spirit distinctly and expressly declares that in latter times some will turn away from the faith, giving attention to deluding and seducing spirits and doctrines that demons teach through the hypocrisy and pretensions of liars whose consciences are seared (cauterized)... (1 Tim. 4:1-2, Amplified).

If our consciences are seared and deadened by stubborn selfishness or habitual sin, spiritual principles will become clouded and indistinct to us. When that happens, our consciences will boldly contradict the revealed Word and will of God.

That's what happened to a man who once came to me for counseling. "God told me to divorce my wife and to go live with another woman," he declared, blatantly ignoring all God's commandments and biblical principles to the contrary. It didn't take long to discover that it wasn't my counsel he was seeking, but my consent and approval. (He got neither, by the way.)

Paul's conscience bore him witness in the Holy Spirit and served as an inner guide because his conscience was clear and upright before God and man. His own testimony bears this out: "I have lived before God, doing my duty with *a perfectly good conscience* until this very day" (Acts 23:1, Amplified, italics mine).

Does this mean that we must be perfect if we want to hear God's voice? No, it simply means that we must strive to walk in love, forgiveness and obedience.

In ourselves, we can never be good enough or strong enough. We must rely upon the living Spirit of God manifested through our lives. If we don't rely upon His strength and righteousness, all our will power and intellectual, physical and emotional strength will not enable us to know and obey God's voice.

God places some things off limits. But He does not withhold those things from us in order to make us feel frustrated and unfulfilled; instead, He has our highest and best interests in mind. That's why He, like any good father, warns His children not to do certain things.

When our first child, John Aaron, was just a toddler, my wife, Melva, and I took him with us to a pizza parlor. The waitress sat our pizza on the table and turned to go. But just then, Melva and I thought of something else we needed. As we talked to the waitress, I happened to glance around just in time to see little John Aaron reaching for the hot pizza.

"No, John!" I yelled. "Don't touch it!" But it was too late. Before I could stop him, he had grabbed a handful of the hot, bubbling cheese and blistered his tiny hand. Instantly, he screamed in pain.

Why did I yell, "No! Don't!"? Because I didn't want him to have any pizza? No, I didn't want him to be burned. There are certain times in your life when God warns, "No! Don't do it!" When that happens, don't misunderstand and think that He's trying to restrict you or keep you from enjoying life.

When your heavenly Father says no, remember that it is always for your good. In addition to other intended benefits, He is protecting you from weights that could hinder you from running your spiritual race. He is trying to keep you from committing sins that could cause your spirit to deteriorate or that would dull your spiritual hearing. (See Heb. 12:1-2.)

However, if we choose habitually to ignore His voice, disobey His warning and sin deliberately, God closes His mouth and ceases to speak. He will not tell us what we want to hear, for He will not give revelation or instruction that violates His Word.

But that may not be the end of it. When we rebel against God's commands and His voice stops speaking in our ears, we may begin hearing other voices which are not of God. You see, Samuel warned:

> Rebellion is as the sin of witchcraft, and stubbornness is as iniquity and idolatry (1 Sam. 15:23).

When we put something ahead of God, whether it be a sin or some desire, it is as if we set up an idol in our hearts. And God warns:

> Everyone...who sets up his idols in his heart, and puts before him what causes him to stumble into iniquity, and then comes to the prophet, I the Lord will answer him who comes, *according to the multitude of his idols* (Ezek. 14:4, italics mine).

Why is such rebellious idolatry so dangerous? The spirit that motivates us to worship those idols, not the Holy Spirit, will begin speaking to us. Because it speaks in the same spiritual sphere and dimension as the voice of the Holy Spirit, we may think it is God's voice. But if we obey that voice, it will deceive us and lead us away from God's perfect plan for our lives.

I cannot overemphasize the importance of reading, knowing and obeying the Word of God. If you reject the principles and commands in God's Word, please don't seek voices, because what you hear will not be God's voice speaking to you. Your human desires and reasoning will rationalize and tell you what you want to hear. Demonic forces will whisper half-truths in your ear and try to get you to compromise what you know is right. But don't expect to hear God speaking to you until you obey the things He has already told you to do.

Therefore, strive to maintain a tender, sensitive con-science. Read and obey the Word of God. Repent and ask forgiveness the moment you realize that you have sinned. As you keep your conscience clear and tender before God, it will bear witness with the Holy Spirit and serve as a safe, sure guide.

Neglect

A fifth hindrance to hearing the voice of God is neglect. As a matter of fact, neglect can be deadly in any relation-ship. I learned that fact the hard way.

The first year we were married, Melva and I lived in a small mobile home behind the church where I served as minister of youth and evangelism. I didn't know when to say no to my own people, so I was constantly run-ning here and there. Not realizing how badly Melva and I needed time alone together, I'd frequently invite two dozen or more kids to our home at a time for snacks and fellowship.

On top of all that, Melva didn't know how to cook, and she was just learning to keep house. You see, Melva was her parents' only child. For over twenty years they had sought God for a baby. They promised Him that if they had a son, they would dedicate him to be a minister, or, if they had a daughter, they would dedicate her to God to become a minister's wife.

Consequently, when Melva was born, her folks kept their promise. They gave her years and years of piano and voice lessons so she would make a good pastor's wife, but they forgot that it would also come in handy if Melva knew how to cook!

I'll never forget the scrambled eggs she made for me when we were first married. Not realizing that part of the plastic spatula she had used to stir the eggs had melted into them, she proudly served up a plate of the *chewiest* scrambled eggs I'd ever sunk my teeth into. But don't worry. I had the good sense to eat them anyway. (I also had the good sense to claim a double dose of divine health and protection with every mouthful.)

But back to the story. Melva was so busy learning to cook, keep house and entertain company and I was so busy ministering at the church and working on my master's degree that we were also busy neglecting each other. After a few months of that foolishness, I realized we weren't spending enough time together.

I came strolling into the house one afternoon in an amorous mood, but Melva was running around dusting, sweeping and cooking, trying to get ready for the company I had invited over. For some reason, she just wasn't interested in hugs and kisses right then.

My offended, 21-year-old male ego decided that it was time for me to put my foot down. So I walked toward the bedroom, raised my voice and ordered: "Melva Jo, you leave all that stuff alone and come on in here with me."

Melva burst out crying, and, just about that time, the Holy Spirit raised His voice to me. He ordered: "Son, *you* come on in here with *Me!*"

I walked into the tiny bedroom I used as a study, shut the door and sat down. The Lord said, "The reason your wife is so busy and is neglecting *you* is that you have been so busy and have been neglecting *Me*."

Well, when the Lord and I got through with our talk, I stumbled boo-hooing into the kitchen, took my wife in my arms and sobbed, "Oh, Melva, I'm so sorry...I'm so sorry."

I hadn't been *rejecting* the Lord; I had just slipped into

the dangerous habit of *neglecting* Him. Can you iden-
tify with what I'm saying?

Martha, the busy, bustling sister of Mary, neglected the
privilege of communing with Jesus for everyday activities
like cooking and cleaning. She got so busy serving Jesus
that she had no time for sitting at His feet. In Luke 10:40,
when Martha complained, "Lord, is it nothing to You
that my sister has left me to serve alone? Tell her then
to help me—to lend a hand and do her part along with
me," Jesus replied:

> Martha, Martha, you are anxious and troubled
> about many things; there is need of (but a few
> things, or) only one. Mary has chosen the good
> portion—that which is to advantage—which shall
> not be taken away from her (Luke 10:41-42,
> Amplified).

Before we get too pious and condemn Martha, maybe
we need to examine our priorities to see if we're guilty
of the same thing.

I believe that one of the greatest sins is not necessarily rejecting God's great salvation, but simply neglecting
it. The author of Hebrews asked, "...how shall we escape
if we *neglect* so great a salvation...?" (Heb. 2:3, italics
mine).

That question was addressed to believers, not unbelievers. We should ask ourselves some similar questions. For instance, "If I neglect communion with God
and don't make knowing and hearing His voice a top
priority, how will I escape Satan's deception in these trying days? How will I live a life directed and empowered
by the Spirit of God?" How, indeed?

In a world where productivity and activity are sometimes equated with spirituality, it's hard to set aside

quality time every day to pray and commune with God. But what is the alternative? Dangerous, deadly neglect. A weakened, deteriorating spirit. Deception. Destruction. On the other hand, there have been very few times when I have chosen to sit at Christ's feet that He, in turn, has not opened my ears so that I could hear His voice.

If we want to hear God's voice, we must repent of the sin of neglect. We must spend quality time with Him daily. As we do, He will give us ears that hear.

Summing It Up

In this chapter, we studied two more hindrances to hearing the voice of God: a calloused conscience and neglect.

1. *A calloused conscience.* Your conscience is the voice of your human spirit. When the Holy Spirit bears witness with your obedient, sensitive conscience, you have a safe, sure guide to the will and purpose of God. However, if you willfully rebel against the Word of God and violate your conscience, you open up yourself to voices of deception and destruction. That is why a tender, sensitive conscience is so important.

2. *Neglect.* Neglecting God's salvation and presence can be just as serious as rejecting them, for either choice leads to deterioration and destruction. As we choose to set aside quality time each day and then "sit at Christ's feet," He will open our ears to hear His voice.

Personal Growth Activity 4

1. Which of these two obstacles to hearing God gives you the greatest problem?

_____ A calloused conscience   _____ Neglect

THE HEARING EAR

2. What definite steps will you take to remove this hindrance?

_____

_____

_____

_____

_____

_____

SECTION THREE

Using God's "Hearing Aids"

CHAPTER FIVE

The Word of God

I've never been too popular with "religious" people. Take one of my seminary professors, for example. I was a senior at the time, and I happened to believe the Bible we were studying. So you can imagine my disappointment one day in class when I heard the professor say something like: "Now, we're not sure about the first eleven chapters of Genesis. We know that the doctrines in that part of the Bible are true, but we can't tell if the people and events described in these chapters were real, historical people and events."

I raised my hand (as I was sometimes known to do in seminary) and said, "Sir, I believe that Jesus thought those people and events were real. In Luke 17 Jesus talked about a man named Noah, an ark and a flood. I believe that Paul thought these people were real. In his Epistles, he talked about Adam and Eve and how sin entered the world through them." (See Rom. 5:12-14; 1 Tim. 2:13-14.)

"Sir," I continued respectfully, "since that's the case, what are we supposed to do with the Gospels, Paul's letters, John 3:16 or with anything else in the Bible that you want to try to fudge on just a little bit?"

As I said, I've never been too popular with "religious" people. But I believe that because God has seen me take my stand for the Bible over and over, He has put me into a place where I can really preach the Bible to His church.

I do believe the Bible, but that's not enough. It's one thing to believe the Bible, but it's another thing to feed upon the Word of God and allow it to perform its wonderful work within us.

I believe that my dedication to the Scriptures is the primary reason God has graced me with ears to hear. Many people don't hear God because they rarely take the time to read, feed and meditate upon the Word of God.

In this third section, I want to talk to you about your Bible and how important it is in learning to hear the voice of God.

First, let's call to mind a few of the wonderful functions of the Word of God.

What the Word of God Does for Us

The Word of God heals. The psalmist said:

> He sent His word and healed them, and delivered them from their destructions (Ps. 107:20).

Solomon wrote:

> My son, attend to my words; consent and submit to my sayings. Let them not depart from your sight; keep them in the center of your heart. For they are life to those who find them, healing and health to all their flesh (Prov. 4:20-22, Amplified).

We are quickened by God's Word. The psalmist prayed, "My earthly life cleaves to the dust; *revive and stimulate me* according to Your word!" (Ps. 119:25, Amplified, italics mine).

70

God's Word strengthens. David said, "My life dissolves and weeps itself away for heaviness; raise me up and strengthen me according to [the promises of] Your Word" (Ps. 119:28, Amplified).

God's Word gives understanding and deliverance. The psalmist prayed:

> Let my mournful cry and supplication come near before You, O Lord; give me understanding— discernment and comprehension—according to Your word [of assurance and promise]. Let my supplication come before You; deliver me according to Your word! (Ps. 119:169,170, Amplified).

God's Word sanctifies us. Jesus prayed, "Sanctify them by Your truth. Your word is truth" (John 17:17).

The Word of God has saving power. James commanded: "So get rid of all uncleanness and the rampant outgrowth of wickedness, and in a humble (gentle, modest) spirit receive and welcome the Word which implanted and rooted [in your hearts] contains the power to save your souls" (James 1:21, Amplified).

As you can see, even a simple survey of the power and functions of the Word of God leaves discerning readers shaking their heads in awe. Is it any wonder that Paul said to Timothy, "Every Scripture is God-breathed— given by His inspiration..." (2 Tim. 3:16, Amplified)?

Jesus Himself has promised: "Heaven and earth will pass away, but My words will by no means pass away" (Matt. 24:35). The Word of God is powerful and life-giving, and it will abide forever.

God's Word Prepares Us

If we want to develop hearing ears, we must learn to cherish and meditate upon the Word of God, for it prepares us in at least six ways to hear His voice.

The Bible Teaches the Basic Doctrines of God

By studying the Bible, we learn the basic doctrines of God: the fall of humanity; Christ's deity and humanity; the atonement and its application; the church and the sacraments; prophecy concerning the last days; the unseen spiritual world; the resurrection of the body; the kingdom of God; and so forth. By reading and seeking to understand the overall teachings of God's Word, we receive general revelation and are grounded in the truth. We will not readily fall victim to false doctrine and error.

On the other hand, if we neglect the study of God's Word, we become targets for seducing spirits and are easily led astray. Consequently, when Satan or his cohorts come to us masquerading as angels of light, peddling lies and half-truths, we cannot discern truth from error. (See 2 Cor. 11:13-15.)

Never forget that Scripture has higher authority than the revelation of any person, church or denomination. If any other gospel than the gospel of the New Testament is preached to you, reject it immediately, no matter how attractive it may be or how good it may feel. Paul warned the Galatians: "But even if we, or an angel from heaven, preach any other gospel to you than what we have preached to you, let him be accursed" (Gal. 1:8).

We would be wise also to receive the warning and counsel of Paul to Timothy:

> But evil men and impostors will grow worse and worse, deceiving and being deceived. But as for you, continue in the things which you have learned and been assured of, knowing from whom you have learned them, and that from childhood you have known the Holy Scriptures, which are

able to make you wise for salvation through faith which is in Christ Jesus. All Scripture is given by inspiration of God, and is profitable for *doctrine*, for reproof, for correction, for instruction in righteousness (2 Tim. 3:13-16, italics mine).

Did you notice Paul's emphasis upon doctrine? Don't be afraid to delve into the deeper things of God. Cherish the Word of God and learn what it teaches. Saturate your mind with its truth. Let the Holy Spirit, the One who wrote the book, teach and instruct you. Then when misguided people or lying spirits speak, you will not be deceived and led astray.

The Word of God Tunes Your Spirit

I read the Bible not only for instruction, but also for "tuning." Let me explain what I mean. Piano tuners use a small, steel, two-pronged tuning fork. When struck, it vibrates at a fixed, constant, known rate, making a musical tone of a certain pitch. Any piano keys that have slipped out of tune can be adjusted according to the true and unchanging pitch of the tuning fork. The Word of God is like a tuning fork. Its pitch is constant.

As we read and study God's Word, our spiritual ears learn to listen for the same tone. As we stay in pitch with the Spirit, voices or messages containing any mixture of error or deception sound off-key to us. When compared with the fixed, constant tone of the Word of God, those messages register in our spirits as "sharp" or "flat."

That's what I mean by saying that I read the Bible not only for instruction, but also for tuning. By saturating my mind in the Word of God, I tune my spiritual ears. I may not receive earth-jarring revelation every time I open the Bible, but my ears are being tuned to His voice and to truth.

John recorded these words of Jesus: "...when He, the Spirit of truth, has come, He will guide you into all truth" (John 16:13). Then in John 17:17, Christ said, "Sanctify them by Your truth. Your word is truth." As we read the Word of God, it sanctifies us and keeps our spiritual ears tuned to the truth. But if we neglect God's Word, we'll be "tone deaf" and dull of hearing.

Let's examine this matter of "tuning" from a slightly different perspective. One night several of my administrative assistants and I were driving out of New Orleans after attending a meeting there. We were trying to listen to the World Series on the radio, but the signal kept fading in and out.

You've had similar experiences. Have you ever wanted to listen to some special program on the car radio, but static and interference made you keep turning the knob back and forth until you got tuned in to that particular station's signal? Or have you ever scanned the dial, searching futilely for a favorite FM station, only to discover that your radio was set on AM? The station was broadcasting, but your radio was just not receiving.

Similar difficulties can arise in the spirit world. God still speaks; He has never ceased, so if we are not hearing His voice, there must be a problem. (And we can rest assured that the problem is not with Him!) Perhaps God is on "FM," and we are on "AM." Or maybe unbelief, sin or ignorance is "jamming the signal," interfering with our reception. Maybe our antenna needs adjusting. If we want to have hearing ears, we must discover the problem and do whatever is necessary to correct it.

Some may say, "I understand what you're saying. I'm beginning to see why reading and studying the Bible are so important. But I don't know how to go about it." If that is your problem, perhaps these pointers will help.

Begin reading the Bible systematically. Several methods have been devised for reading the Bible through in one year. For instance, if you read three chapters daily and five chapters on Sunday (or whatever day you choose), you can read the Bible through in a year. I challenge you to find the method that best suits you and use it to read the Bible through systematically in a twelve-month period.

One new convert, who had vowed to read the Bible through but got "bogged down" in the Old Testament genealogies, joked: "The Bible is a book full of big names busy begetting other big names!" If you're a new Christian and that's the way you feel, you might prefer to begin your Bible reading with the Gospel of John, then go on to the book of Acts, the Psalms and Proverbs.

The important thing is to form the habit of reading the Word of God daily. Then, when you're ready, begin at Genesis and add five or ten minutes of systematic reading to your daily time of devotional Bible reading.

Some may say, "I've tried to read the Bible through, but I didn't understand it." If that is your problem, look through several of the newer translations or paraphrases of the Bible and choose one that you can understand.

Others may say,"I don't have time to read the Bible." To that group I ask: "But do you have time to read the newspaper or watch the news? Do you spend any time during the day or evening watching television or visiting on the phone with friends? Do you take time to exercise your body? Do you take time to eat two or three meals a day?"

Do you see what I'm getting at? I'd rather fast one meal a day and spend that time reading my Bible than eat two or three meals a day and neglect the Word of God. That's how important the Word of God is to me. Christians had better get serious about this, my friend.

It's a fact. While the devil is working overtime to kill, steal and destroy, lazy believers are spending multiplied hours every week sprawled in a recliner, drinking diet Coke and watching television. They pray and read the Bible only when it's convenient, then they wonder why their marriages are breaking up and why they're losing their kids or going bankrupt. It's time for every believer to develop a systematic plan of Bible reading.

Begin to read the Bible spiritually. How can you read the Bible "spiritually"? As you are reading, keep a prayerful, attentive heart. Ask God to speak to you as you read the Word. Keep your ears open and in tune with His voice. Sometimes He will have a special word for you, and sometimes He won't, but just keep reading, regardless. We all need the tuning. We all need instruction in righteousness.

Often I ask, "Holy Spirit, is there anything in particular that You want me to read? If so, lead me to those passages." Many times over the years, the Spirit of God has done just that. Sometimes He has told me to turn to a certain book of the Bible. Other times, He has given me the exact reference. Sometimes He has inspired me to study a particular subject.

All believers should get into the habit of asking the Spirit to direct them to "the word in the Word" that they need. The Holy Spirit knows the book from cover to cover; after all, He wrote it. He also knows your circumstances. He knows what's ahead of you tomorrow or next week. Ask the Holy Spirit to prepare your heart to hear His voice and to lead you into truth.

Read the Bible expectantly. As you read the Bible, expect God to talk to you either through the teaching of the Scripture or by highlighting a particular passage.

Have you ever had a verse just "jump off the page" at you? I have. It's one thing to read the Bible, but it's another thing when it reads us! Learn to read the Bible expectantly. Keep a pencil and notebook or prayer diary nearby so you can jot down what God says to you.

Make the commitment to study the Bible each day: systematically, spiritually and expectantly. As you do, it will tune your spiritual ears to know and understand the voice of God.

The Bible Confirms the Spirit's Leading

The Bible not only instructs us in basic doctrines and tunes our spirits, it also confirms the leading of the Holy Spirit.

Have you ever sought God for confirmation as to some specific action or direction you should take? Has God then spoken to you through His Word, confirming what you should do? If not, I want to encourage you to ask God to confirm through the Scriptures the Holy Spirit's leadings.

But, when a voice of uncertain origin speaks in your spirit telling you to do a certain thing, wait and obey it only when God confirms that leading through His Word.

May I give you a "for instance"? I was a student at Dallas Baptist College when I met a cute little gal named Melva Jo Bryant. I liked the way she looked, sang, smiled, walked and talked. In other words, one look at Melva Jo was enough to make my bells jingle, and it wasn't even Christmas.

Melva was single, and I was single but there was a problem—me. I didn't want to get married. I had my heart set on becoming the next apostle Paul. So every time the verse, "Rejoice with the wife of thy youth" (Prov. 5:18, KJV), bobbed to the surface in my spirit, I would push it back under and mutter, "I rebuke you, Satan!"

But the happy little thought that splashed and laughed so playfully inside me was undaunted by my fierce rebukes. As I prayed harder and harder about Melva, the impression grew stronger and stronger until I couldn't push it under or ignore it any longer. It was then I realized that God wanted Melva Jo Bryant to become Mrs. Larry Lea. After that, all I had to do was seek God's timing and direction and court her.

The psalmist declared,

> Your word is a lamp to my feet
> And a light to my path (Ps. 119:105).

He also testified:

> The law of the Lord is perfect, restoring the [whole] person; the testimony of the Lord is sure, making wise the simple. The precepts of the Lord are right, rejoicing the heart; the commandment of the Lord is pure and bright, enlightening the eyes...Moreover by them is Your servant warned [reminded, illuminated and instructed]; and in keeping them there is great reward (Ps. 19:7-8,11, Amplified).

And Solomon promised:

> When you go, it [the Word of your parents' God] shall lead you; when you sleep, it shall keep you, and when you waken, it shall talk with you. For the commandment is a lamp, and the whole teaching of the law is light, and reproofs of discipline are the way of life... (Prov. 6:22,23, Amplified).

As you give yourself to reading and studying God's Word, the Lord will speak over and over to you through the Scriptures. When you receive a confirmation from the Scriptures and a verse "goes off" inside you like fireworks on the Fourth of July, confirming the leading of the Holy Spirit, nobody will have to tell you what happened. You will know that it's God.

The Word of God Washes Your Inner Man

I'm sure you've had an experience similar to the one I'm about to describe. You've been out in the world all day, wrestling with all kinds of spirits and warding off the spiritual assaults of the enemy as he has bombarded your eyes, ears and mind with a hand-picked variety of temptations and pressures. When you get home, you feel as if you need a spiritual bath. What do you do?

May I suggest that you *not* plop down in front of the television set. That's like a hog jumping back into the mud. You and I may as well face the fact that we're not going to get clean by watching television; instead, we must take a spiritual bath. We must let the Word of God wash our minds and cleanse our spirits, as water cleanses our bodies.

Paul reminded the Ephesians: "...Christ loved the church and gave Himself up for her, so that He might sanctify her, having *cleansed* her by the *washing of water with the Word...*" (Eph. 5:25-26, Amplified, italics mine).

And Jesus said to His disciples, "You are already clean because of the word which I have spoken to you" (John 15:3).

Let me ask you a question. If you could look into a spiritual mirror, would the face you see be "squeaky clean" and fresh, or would you see a filthy, grimy face peering back at you? The Word of God is the "soap and water" that washes the grime and stench of the world off us. The evening news won't do it. "As the World Burns" won't do it. We must take a spiritual bath in the

79

Word of God every day.

The Word of God Defeats the Devil

The Word of God not only instructs, tunes and washes us, it also enables us consistently to defeat the devil. When the devil came to Christ in the wilderness to tempt Him, Jesus did not pray. He did not praise. He did not bind or loose. No, He spoke the Word of God, and Satan retreated. It is the same for us today. The Word of God is our offensive weapon against the devil.

I believe there is a word in the Word for every situation of life. When the enemy comes to me and says, "You are weak," I know that the Word of God says, "Let the weak say, 'I am strong' " (Joel 3:10). When the devil says, "You are poor," I reply, "Devil, I am rich because of what the Lord has done for me. My God shall supply all my need according to His riches in glory by Christ Jesus." (See Phil. 4:19.) If the enemy says, "You are sick," I tell him, "No, I'm not. By Christ's stripes I am healed." (See Is. 53:5.) Are you catching on? When the devil attacks, stab him with the sharp, two-edged sword of the Word. (See Eph. 6:17.)

In the wilderness, each time the devil tried to tempt Jesus with twisted half-truths wrested out of context from the Scriptures, Jesus turned the situation around by quoting an appropriate Scripture from God's Word. (See Luke 4:3-12.)

Believers not well-grounded in God's Word may have trouble with the devil planting doubts in their minds: "You're not saved. You're not really born again. Your experience wasn't real." When that happens, what should they do?

First of all, they should not rely on some emotional experience they have had. They should not try to analyze how much faith they had when they tried to believe or wonder if they prayed all the words in the "sinners' prayer" just exactly right. Instead, they should turn to the Word of God and quote to the devil the words of the beloved apostle John: "These things I have written to you who believe in the name of the Son of God, that you may *know* that you have eternal life, and that you may continue to believe in the name of the Son of God" (1 John 5:13, italics added).

John said that if you believe in Jesus, you have eternal life. Tell that to the devil. And while you're at it, read Titus 3:5 to him: "Not by works of righteousness which we have done, but according to His mercy He saved us, through the washing of regeneration and renewing of the Holy Spirit." Do you know what that does to the devil? It puts him in reverse!

Can we talk? Can we really get "real" about this matter of doubts? While I was in Bible college, the devil attacked me with doubts about my salvation. I was already preaching. I'd already spoken in tongues. I'd already been baptized in water—a couple of times. But the enemy tormented me with doubts, saying, "You're not really saved. Maybe you need to go through it all one more time, just to make sure."

Can you relate to that? Has the devil ever tormented you with doubts about your salvation, a healing, a promise from God? If he's played that little game with you, then you probably already know what I had to do to get rid of him and his nasty lies.

One day I'd had enough of it. Determined not to let him steal another inch of spiritual ground from me, I planted my feet, squared my shoulders and declared: "Satan, the Bible says that my salvation is a gift from God. I didn't deserve it, and I can't earn it. I've accepted that gift, and God will never take away from me what He freely gave to me in the first place."

Oh, the devil stood there and resisted me for a while, but I refused to discuss my feelings or failures. Instead, I just kept poking him with the Word of God. After a while, he got sick of hearing about the blood of Jesus, the gift of righteousness, my full and free forgiveness, justification, sanctification and the like, and he picked up his little sack of squirming, gnawing doubts, walked away and left me alone.

Our hope must be built on Christ's shed blood and righteousness. We must rest our case in His finished work on the cross and in the changeless Word of God. Don't try to argue your experience with the devil; just keep jabbing him with the Word of God.

Whenever Satan attacks you in any realm—physically, financially, emotionally, spiritually, mentally—find yourself a good analytical concordance to the Bible (Young's or Strong's, for example), look up the verses and promises that apply specifically to your situation and claim them. Quote them. Turn them into prayers and faith declarations. Make them yours. Use them to back the devil down. The Word of God will defeat him every time.

God's Word Feeds Your Spirit Being

Every believer has an inner spirit being. Paul the apostle prayed: "For this reason I bow my knees to the Father of our Lord Jesus Christ...that He would grant you, according to the riches of His glory, to be strengthened with might through His Spirit in *the inner man*" (Eph. 3:14,16, italics mine).

Just as your outer, physical being needs to eat nourishing food to remain strong and healthy, your spirit being needs to feed on spiritual food. Unfortunately, many Christians allow their spirit beings to grow weak, anemic and sickly from lack of nourishment. They ignore Peter's wise counsel: "As newborn babes, desire the pure milk of the word, that you may grow thereby, if indeed you have tested that the Lord is gracious" (1 Pet. 2:2-3).

The Word of God is spiritual food, but many believers don't take time to feed upon it. Then they wonder why they're too weak and defenseless to walk in the Spirit or fight off Satan's attacks.

I've been told that people dying of starvation eventually reach the point where they feel no hunger at all. I'm afraid that many believers are at the point of spiritual starvation; they don't know their severe condition. Their languishing spirits no longer crave the bread of life or the milk of the Word. They don't even know they're dying. To such believers, Christ issues this urgent invitation:

> Wait and listen, every one who is thirsty! Come to the waters; and he who has no money, come, buy and eat! Yes, come, but priceless [spiritual] wine and milk without money and without price [simply for the self-surrender that accepts the blessing].
>
> Why do you spend your money for that which is not bread? And your earnings for what does not satisfy? Hearken diligently to me, and eat what is good, and let your soul delight itself in fatness [the profuseness of spiritual joy].
>
> Incline your ear [submit and consent to the Divine will], and come to Me; hear, and your soul shall revive... (Is. 55:1-3, Amplified).

Let's look at 2 Timothy 3:16-17: "All Scripture is given by inspiration of God, and is profitable for doctrine, for reproof, for correction, for instruction in righteousness, that the man of God may be complete, thoroughly equipped for every good work.''

Do you know what these verses say to me regarding the spiritual food of the Word? These verses tell me that the Word of God is a perfectly balanced diet. It contains exactly what you and I need to be complete, thoroughly equipped, healthy and strong. The words of faith and the good doctrine of the Word of God nourish and strengthen us. (See 1 Tim. 4:6.) Have you tasted the good Word of God lately? (See Heb. 6:5.)

Many believers are familiar with the often-told story of the white dog and the black dog, but just in case you might not have heard it, let me share it.

It seems that a backwoodsman in Alaska came into town every so often to replenish his supplies, make a round of the local bars and gamble a little. The man always arranged dog fights, pitting one of his savage, black sled dogs against a rugged, white dog he owned, and he took bets on the outcomes.

Noticing that the backwoodsman seemed to have an uncanny knack for betting on the winning dog, a friend asked to know his secret. "No secret," replied the backwoodsman with a grin and a wink. "It's simple. I always know ahead of time when I'll have to be coming into town to fetch supplies. Several days before I arrive I starve the *white* dog, if I want the *black* dog to win. Or I starve the *black* dog, if I want the *white* dog to win."

Have you been wondering why your *spirit* is losing so many rounds in its fight against the *flesh*? Maybe you ought to check it out. Are you feeding your spirit being, enabling it to grow mighty and strong? Or are you, by neglecting the Word of God, starving and weakening your spirit being, rendering him no match for savage, spiritual enemies?

But that's not the only consequence of neglecting God's Word. Luke 16:10-11 contains a thought-provoking statement from Jesus Himself:

> He who is faithful in what is least is faithful also in much; and he who is unjust in what is least is unjust also in much. Therefore if you have not been faithful in the unrighteous mammon, who will commit to your trust the true riches?

If you and I want God to communicate with us on a day-to-day basis and entrust us with further revelation, we must be faithful and consistent in our daily Bible study. If we are not faithful and obedient to the truths God has already put into our hands, why in the world should He trust us with more?

The Bible is God's primary method for revealing His nature, His character and His basic doctrinal truths. The Word of God is also His instrument for cleansing, edifying, strengthening and feeding. But that's not all. You see, God also uses the Bible to "test" us. Through our obedient attentiveness and devotion to the Word of God or through our careless disregard and neglect of the Scriptures, God determines who is worthy to be entrusted with true spiritual riches. We are all being tested. How about you? Are you failing or passing?

If you are not taking time each day to read and study the Word of God, you are missing out on one of the most exciting, enriching experiences in a believer's life. Two New Testament disciples said it like this: "Did not our heart burn within us while He talked with us on the road, and while He opened the Scriptures to us?" (Luke 24:32).

If you will do your part, setting aside time each day to read and meditate upon the Word, Christ will do His part. He will open your heart, allowing you to pay attention to and understand His Word. Your heart will burn within you as the great Teacher Himself enlightens your understanding and reveals the wonderful truths of the Bible. And I'd guess that, before long, the mean, old, black dog of your flesh will think twice before trying to pick a fight with your spirit!

Summing It Up

What are the main points to remember from this lesson and put into practice? First of all, we need to rededicate our lives to reading and meditating upon the Word of God. As we do, God's Word will prepare us in at least six ways to hear His voice:

1. *The Word of God instructs us in the basic doctrines of God.* As we read and understand the overall teaching of God's Word, we are grounded in the truth. We will not easily fall victim to false doctrine and error.

2. *The Word of God tunes our spirits.* As we read the Bible, it tunes our spiritual ears to the things of the Spirit. It enables us to distinguish truth from error and to recognize the voice of the flesh and of Satan, for those voices will not "resonate" in our spirits, as does the voice of the Spirit of God.

3. *God's Word confirms what He has been speaking in our spirits.* If we wait upon Him and consistently read and study the Scriptures, God will confirm through His Word what the Holy Spirit has been telling our spirits.

4. *God's Word washes our inner person.* We should take a daily spiritual "bath" in the Word of God. Its sanctifying truths will wash and cleanse our spirits from the filth and grime of the world.

5. *The Word of God consistently defeats the devil.* When the devil tries to trap or tempt us, we should poke him with the sword of the Spirit, the Word of God. We

must learn to answer his lying accusations with what the Bible says, not with our past experiences or by intellectual reasoning.

6. *God's Word feeds our spirit-being.* If we want to be mighty in spirit, we must learn to nourish our inner being by feeding upon the perfectly balanced diet of the Word of God.

If we neglect His precious Word, God will not count you and me as good candidates for revelation. But by consistently reading and studying the Word of God, we are saying: *God, I'm being faithful. I am not neglecting what You have put in my hand. I cherish Your revelation. I treasure Your words and Your will. Teach me. May Your holy Word prepare my spiritual ears to hear Your voice. Speak to me, Lord. I am listening.*

When you get to the place where you are praying prayers like that, get ready—you're about to hear God's voice!

Personal Growth Activity 5

Reflecting personally on the points presented in chapter five, complete the following sentences:

1. I had never realized that _____
_____
_____
_____

2. This thought had a significant impact upon me: _____
_____
_____
_____
_____

3. I am truly sorry that _____
_____
_____
_____
_____

THE HEARING EAR

4. One thing I plan to begin doing immediately is _____
_____
_____
_____
_____

CHAPTER SIX

Praying in the Spirit

I was visiting a large denominational church in Dallas when one of the members cornered me. "Larry Lea, let me get this straight about you," he said in an authoritative tone. "You have a B.A. degree from Dallas Baptist University. Right?"

Not knowing which direction this conversation was about to take, I smiled and nodded my head.

"You have an 88-semester-hour master of divinity degree from Southwestern Baptist Theological Seminary, don't you?" he asked.

"Right," I replied with another nod.

"And you've had two doctoral degrees conferred upon you. Is that right?" he prodded, staring me right in the eye.

"Yes, sir, that's correct."

"Then, man," he exclaimed, his expression a mixture of bewilderment and frustration, "why in this world do you speak in *tongues*?"

I couldn't keep the smile off my face as I replied, "Because I'm normal."

Caught a little off guard, he turned his head slightly,

cocked one eyebrow and looked at me out of the corner of his eyes. "Normal according to *what*?" he asked warily.

"Not normal according to your religious tradition or to the religious tradition I was brought up in," I said, "but normal according to the Scriptures."

Was I right? Is speaking in tongues, "praying with the spirit" (or by the Holy Spirit within us) as Paul called it in 1 Corinthians 14:14-15, normal according to the Scriptures? Let me share a few of the facts I've uncovered on the subject, and you can decide for yourself.

In every one of the Gospels, Jesus is introduced as the baptizer in the Holy Spirit. (See Matt. 3:11; Mark 1:8; Luke 3:16; John 1:33.) Jesus is both Savior and baptizer, yet most of us have been taught to appropriate Him only as Savior.

The Bible contains a great deal of Scripture on the prophesied outpouring of the Holy Spirit in the last days—speaking in tongues and praying and ministering in the Spirit. (See Is. 28:11-12; Joel 2:28-29; Christ's words in Mark 16:17; Acts 2:4; Acts 10:44-48; Acts 19:2-6 and 1 Cor. 12-14, for example.) Actually, more has been written in the Word of God on this subject, tongues, than on communion or some of the other church ordinances.

"The doctrine of baptisms" is the third of the doctrinal foundational principles listed in Hebrews 6:1-2. Notice that the author of Hebrews says "baptisms," indicating that there is more than one baptism. What are those baptisms?

Baptism by the Holy Spirit into the body of Christ is one of three distinct baptisms mentioned in the New Testament. This baptism is synonymous with the salvation experience which occurs when one repents from dead works and by faith receives Jesus Christ as Savior and Lord. This is the baptism of which Paul spoke in 1 Corinthians 12:13: "For by one Spirit we were all baptized into one body—whether we be Jews or Greeks, whether slaves or free—and all have been made to drink into one Spirit."

Water baptism is another of the three baptisms referred to in Hebrews 6. New Testament Christians considered water baptism an important part of their profession of faith. Paul taught that water baptism represents spiritual circumcision from flesh-controlled to Spirit-controlled living. (See Rom. 6:1-14.)

Baptism in the Holy Spirit is still another baptism experienced by New Testament believers. It was preached as a baptism distinct from the others. John the Baptist prophesied: "I indeed baptize you with water unto repentance, but He who is coming after me is mightier than I...He will baptize you with the Holy Spirit and fire" (Matt. 3:11). Peter declared: "Repent, and let every one of you be baptized in the name of Jesus Christ for the remission of sins; and you shall receive the gift of the Holy Spirit" (Acts 2:38).

In 1 Corinthians 14 Paul discusses in great detail the exact purposes for speaking in tongues. He describes the gift of tongues along with the gift of interpretation, to be used in the public service (vv. 5-13,26-28,39). He mentions tongues as a sign to the unbeliever (vv. 21-22). And the apostle also discusses the ministry of the Holy Spirit in assisting believers in their personal prayer and private communion with God (vv. 2,4; see also Rom. 8:26-27).

Yet many denominations and ministers have cautiously, deliberately steered clear of this important subject. By denying their followers—who are *spiritual beings*—the reality of the communion and power of the

91

Holy Spirit, they have created a tremendous vacuum, a deep craving for fulfillment and reality, that cries out to be filled. That is why I believe much of the blame for rampant drug and alcohol abuse, lust and greed, and the growth of the occult, Eastern religions and cults can be placed at the door of the church.

Why Tongues?

Why did God need to enable believers to speak in tongues in the first place? To find that answer, we'll have to start at the beginning of God's dealings with man.

In the beginning, Adam and Eve, the beings God created to become the parents of the human race, were blissfully content in the beautiful garden where God had put them. (See Gen. 2.) They walked, talked and fellowshipped with God until they fell for Satan's deceptive lies and chose to rebel against God. (See Gen. 3:1-7.)

God had warned Adam and Eve that they were not to eat of the tree of the knowledge of good and evil, "for in the day that you eat of it you shall surely die" (Gen. 2:17). When Adam and Eve sinned and disobeyed, although their physical bodies did not instantly fall over dead, their spirits, through which they communed with God, died.

To better understand what happened, let's compare Adam to a brightly burning candle in a candlestick. Think of Adam's body as the candlestick and think of Adam's soul—his mind, will and emotions—as the candle itself. Now imagine Adam's spirit as the wick of the candle and think of God's quickening, living presence as the flame.

When Adam chose to transgress God's commandment—to step willfully and deliberately over God's clearly drawn boundary—the Spirit of God was separated from him, and his spirit being died. The living, burning flame of God's presence departed from Adam's (and Eve's) spirit, just as you would blow out a candle, leaving only a smoking, charred wick. The intimate spirit-to-Spirit communion once enjoyed by man and God was destroyed.

The spirit of every individual born into the human race thereafter has been lifeless and dark, uninhabited and unillumined. On the outside, a person's body, along with his mind, will and emotions, seems normal. But on the inside, the spirit being is utterly lifeless, stillborn.

God gave Adam and Eve wonderful minds and a language with which they could communicate with their Creator and with their fellowmen. But they and their descendants used those God-given abilities to help achieve their own selfish, rebellious purposes. Because the majority of mankind was not interested in God's glory or in fulfilling His eternal purposes in the earth, God confused languages at the Tower of Babel. (See Gen. 11:5-9.)

After the fall, unregenerate man learned to rely upon the physical body and upon the mind, will and emotions. He tried to reach God with intellect, good works, and so forth, but these efforts were futile. One misery-plagued generation plodded after another. Sin. Sorrow. Sickness. Guilt. Estrangement. Then God mercifully intervened in the person of Jesus Christ.

When Jesus came to earth, He came in obedience to undo what the first Adam had done through his disobedience. Jesus came to reverse the sin and spiritual death that Adam's fall had brought upon mankind. (See Rom. 5:14; 1 Cor. 15:21,22,45, Amplified.) He came to be the propitiation—the cleansing and life-giving sacrifice of atonement and reconciliation—for man's sin. (See Rom. 3:25, Amplified.) Jesus came to reconcile a banished race to a holy God, to restore the love and fellowship that man and his Maker once knew.

When Jesus is revealed to us as Savior and we confess Christ as Lord, the life of God is breathed into our spirits. It is as if the Creator commands,

Awake, you who sleep, arise from the dead, and Christ will give you light (Eph. 5·14).

Suddenly the wick of man's spirit glows, then bursts into flame as the Holy Spirit comes into the believer and takes up His abode.

But as awesome as that miraculous event may seem, God does not stop there. He has made even deeper, fuller provision for fellowship and communion with mankind.

This Matter of Tongues

The blood of Christ and the prayer language of the Spirit restored to believers the communion with God which Adam and Eve lost. On the day of Pentecost, God gave to the church the pure, uncontaminated love language of the Holy Spirit. With this language believers can communicate directly with God, not only through our limited minds and flawed emotions, but through our born-again spirits.

Now when the Day of Pentecost had fully come, they were all with one accord in one place. And suddenly there came a sound from heaven, as of a rushing mighty wind, and it filled the whole house where they were sitting. Then there appeared to them divided tongues, as of fire, and one sat upon each of them. And they were all filled with the Holy Spirit and began to speak with other tongues, as the Spirit gave them utterance.

Now there were dwelling in Jerusalem Jews, devout men, from every nation under heaven. And when this sound occurred, the multitude came together, and were confused, because everyone heard them speak in his own language.

Then they were all amazed and marveled, saying to one another, "Look, are not all these who speak Galileans? And how is it that we hear, each in our own language in which we were born?.... We hear them speaking in our own tongues the wonderful works of God" (Acts 2:1-8,11).

Then Peter addressed the crowd:

But this is what was spoken by the prophet Joel: "And it shall come to pass in the last days, says God, That I will pour out of My Spirit on all flesh; your sons and your daughters shall prophesy, your young men shall see visions, your old men shall dream dreams. And on My menservants and on My maidservants I will pour out My Spirit in those days; and they shall prophesy..." (Acts. 2:14,16-18).

At the conclusion of Peter's sermon when the crowd yelled, "Men and brethren, what shall we do?" Peter exclaimed:

Repent, and let every one of you be baptized in the name of Jesus Christ for the remission of sins; and you shall receive the gift of the Holy Spirit. For the promise is to you and to your children, *and to all who are afar off, as many as the Lord our God will call* (Acts 2:38-39, italics mine).

God's marvelous gift of the Holy Spirit is still available to every Christian. Just as believers who spoke in tongues were not considered strange or abnormal in the New Testament church, so believers today who pray in the Spirit, releasing their prayer languages to God, are not strange or abnormal to Him.

Yet much of the religious world believes that praying in the Spirit is abnormal. Praying in a language that the mind does not understand or comprehend seems "spooky" or foolish to some who are so dominated by their intellects that they back off from anything that must be spiritually discerned or understood. (See 1 Cor. 2:14.)

But how many of those same people reject things in the natural world that they don't understand? How many of them could totally disassemble their cars, computers and compact disc players and put them back together in perfectly functioning order? How many could construct workable microwave ovens, orbiting space satellites or nationwide telephone systems if necessary? Face it. Not many of them. But their lack of understanding doesn't stop them from using these modern-day marvels, does it? Nor should our inability to comprehend the miraculous gift of tongues prevent our making use of this supernatural means of communicating with God.

Since when did man ever imagine that he could comprehend the mysteries of God anyway? A wise person once observed: "The mind of man is like a tea cup, and the mind of God is like the ocean. Man's little tea cup will never be able to contain God's great, big ocean." Well said!

But when God puts a new spirit within a person and then fills and floods that born-again human spirit with His Holy Spirit, it's as if that person were right back in the Garden of Eden, walking, talking and fellowshipping with his Creator. As man releases his new prayer language to God, he and God can commune spirit to Spirit—totally unhampered by the individual's natural vocabulary or by his ignorant or selfish human desires and reasoning.

The prayer language inspired by the Spirit can be any one of thousands of earthly languages spoken by other races or a heavenly language spoken by angels (1 Cor. 13:1). If He deems it necessary in order to circumvent Satan's plans and purposes, the Spirit can give the believer utterance in a language completely unintelligible to Satan and his demon powers.

Even a brief study of the Scriptures confirms the inestimable value of speaking in tongues. However, believers have often misunderstood the purpose and significance of God's gift.

What Speaking in Tongues Is Not

Because many Christians have been misinformed as to the purpose of speaking in tongues, I want to make very clear what speaking in tongues is *not*!

Speaking in Tongues Is Not Necessary for Salvation

Speaking in tongues is *not* a prerequisite for salvation. The Bible clearly teaches what man must do to be saved, and speaking in tongues is not one of the prerequisites.

> If you confess with your mouth the Lord Jesus and believe in your heart that God has raised Him from the dead, you will be saved. For with the heart one believes to righteousness, and with the mouth confession is made to salvation. For the Scripture says,..."Whoever calls upon the name of the Lord shall be saved" (Rom. 10:9-11,13).

Faith, repentance and making Jesus Lord are necessary for salvation. Speaking in tongues is not.

Speaking in Tongues Does Not Mean Superiority

Speaking in tongues is not a prerequisite for salvation, and neither is it a badge of spiritual superiority. The believers at Corinth spoke in tongues and manifested the gifts of the Spirit, but Paul had to instruct them about spiritual maturity and teach them how to function decently and in order in the Spirit. (See 1 Cor. 14:1,12, 37,39-40.)

Spiritual maturity is not guaranteed just because a believer speaks in tongues. The degree of one's spiritual maturity is gauged by that person's love for God and fellowman, not by any one spiritual gift.

Speaking in Tongues Is Not a Cure-all

Many believers mistakenly believe that speaking in tongues is the final solution to every problem or situation. They forget about other powerful ministrations of the Spirit, such as words of knowledge or wisdom; gifts of healings, miracles, faith and so forth. Ignorant of the Spirit's diversity, they are like a carpenter who carries only a screwdriver in his tool box. A screwdriver is a marvelous tool, but sometimes a hammer and saw, a drill or a tape measure would come in mighty handy!

Do you understand what I'm saying? Of course we should lay hands on people and pray over them in the Spirit. Many deep problems can be relieved and even obliterated by praying in tongues. But sometimes, the Spirit of God will put a different "tool" in our hands if we will let Him. He may want to speak a word of prophecy or a word of knowledge. He may lead us to give a word of exhortation, instruction or rebuke. The person's need may also require the long-term counsel, example or teaching of a mature believer who is qualified to minister in that particular area.

May I carry this just one step further? Many believers,

because of spiritual ignorance or sheer laziness, think of the power of the Holy Spirit as a spiritual short-cut. They kick back, fold their arms across their chests and sigh: "I speak in tongues. Therefore, I don't have to work, study, read, prepare or pray any more. The Holy Ghost is my strength and my wisdom. He is my Advocate and Intercessor. He will do all the work for me." Wrong! You'll not find that teaching in the Bible.

Remember: Speaking in tongues is not a badge of salvation or of spiritual superiority. Neither is it a spiritual short cut or a divine cure-all for every situation.

What Speaking in Tongues Is

According to the Scriptures, after Christ ascended into heaven, God blessed His church with a marvelous gift. On the day of Pentecost He filled believers with His Holy Spirit and gave them a supernatural language with which each one could communicate with Him, spirit to Spirit.

Why should believers today pray in the Spirit? Because the language of the Spirit is untainted by rebellion or selfishness. Because it is a language that allows mortal beings with limited understanding to intercede according to the perfect will of the immortal, all-wise God. (See Rom. 8:26-27.) Because it is a prayer language through which men and women can come into agreement with God's holy purposes and be endued with supernatural ability, efficiency and might to live out and declare those purposes in the earth. (See Acts 1:8, Amplified.) When the spirit of a believer communes with the Creator in the language of the Spirit, like a fish in the water or a bird in the sky, he is in his natural habitat. Like Adam and Eve in the Garden of Eden, he is walking, talking and communicating with God in the "garden" of his heart.

Seven Benefits of Praying in Tongues

First of all, I should make it clear that every believer chooses whether or not he or she will pray in the Spirit. Just as God never makes you repent, believe or witness, He also never makes you speak in tongues. But according to the Word of God, if you choose to pray in tongues on a regular basis, releasing your prayer language to God, you will experience at least seven benefits.

Gifts and Power Are Released in Your Life

On the day of Pentecost, the gifts and power of the Spirit were released in believers gathered in the Upper Room. They were filled with the Holy Spirit and the immediate results were astonishing. For instance, Peter, who had lied, cursed and denied the Lord just before Christ's crucifixion, now stood in front of many of the very Jews who had put Jesus to death and boldly proclaimed a powerful gospel message so anointed that 3,000 people were saved that day.

Where did Peter get such boldness, courage and anointing to witness of Jesus? How was a fisherman able to preach to some of the most educated people of his day and see them converted? There's only one logical explanation. The gifts and power of the Holy Spirit were released in Peter's life when the Spirit of God filled and flooded him and the others as they prayed in the Upper Room.

The New Testament church continued to release the gifts and power of the Spirit. In Acts 3:1-8, Peter and John spoke healing to a man who had been lame from his mother's womb. In Acts 5:3-10, when Peter, by the power and revelation of the Spirit, rebuked Ananias and his wife, Sapphira, for lying to the Holy Ghost, they dropped dead at Peter's feet.

In Acts 5:12-16, Luke records that the Spirit's power continued to be manifested in the church. The apostles performed many signs and wonders among the people; multitudes were saved, healed and delivered; sick people were brought out into the streets in the hope that Peter's shadow might fall upon them and heal them as he passed by!

In Acts 6:8, Stephen, one of seven deacons in the early church, worked great wonders and signs among the people. In Acts 8:5-7, Philip evangelized the city of Samaria, cast out demons and saw many people healed and delivered. Over and over again the New Testament records marvelous examples of what the Holy Spirit did when His gifts and power were released through the lives of believers.

You may be thinking, "Oh, wouldn't it be wonderful to be used of God to see people saved, healed and delivered!" Yes, it would. But I believe that you will never see a full release of the other supernatural gifts of the Holy Spirit in your life until you release your prayer language. The gift of tongues leads you into dimensions of the Spirit that you will never know otherwise.

Some people have been taught that speaking in tongues is the least of the gifts, but the Bible never says that. According to the book of Acts, it was the first spiritual gift bestowed. Speaking in tongues preceded and actually "triggered" the release of the other gifts and manifestations of the Spirit. If you've been taught to believe something different, why not study the Bible and let it interpret and speak for itself? This matter of the gifts and power of the Holy Spirit is too important to take somebody else's word for it.

Open your New Testament and read for yourself. If you sincerely want all that God intends you to have, why not take off your denominational "blinders" and ask the Spirit of God to lead you into all truth? None of us has *all* the truth, but if we are open to the Spirit's leading, we can have more.

Like those New Testament believers, you and I can experience the release of the Spirit's gifts and power through our own lives. We can see multitudes turn to Christ. We, too, can turn our world upside down. (See Acts 17:6.)

Your Spirit Is Edified

A second benefit of praying in tongues is continual edification. The word "edify" (*oikodomeo*) means "to build up"; "to promote spiritual growth."

Since "edify" isn't a word that most of us hear every day, the meaning may seem a little fuzzy. This illustration may clarify the term. Have you ever turned on the key to start your car and heard only an unwelcome growl: a battery that needed to be recharged. When that happens, you need a pair of jumper cables hooked to another power source to "build up" your battery. That's what "edify" means.

Our spiritual "batteries" need to be recharged—built up or edified. How is this accomplished? Paul told the Corinthians, "He who speaks in a tongue edifies himself..." (1 Cor. 14:4).

Some may say, "But I thought that 1 Corinthians 14:12-14 repudiated speaking in tongues." Not so. Paul is not recommending *dis*-use as a cure for the Corinthians' *abuse* of tongues; rather, he is recommending *proper* use. Remember, in that same chapter, Paul also said: "I wish you all spoke with tongues...I thank my God I speak with tongues more than you all...Do not forbid to speak with tongues" (1 Cor. 14:5,18,39). That doesn't sound as if the apostle was repudiating tongues.

Paul knew that he, and every Christian, needed the edifying gift of tongues. Let's face it. Every believer is bombarded by "downers." People put us down; situations make us feel low. Our physical bodies grow weary and age. We constantly look for that something that will build us up. Paul had found that something—or rather, that Someone—and wrote, "He who speaks in a tongue edifies himself."

As this wise apostle said, when we speak in tongues, we build up our spirits, promoting our spiritual growth. Thus edification is a second dynamic result of praying in tongues. The more we pray in tongues, the more we are edified.

The Spirit's Prayer Language Aids Intercession

In 1 Corinthians 14, Paul gives still another result of praying in tongues: "For if I pray in a tongue, my spirit prays, but my understanding is unfruitful. What is the result then? *I will* pray with the spirit, and *I will* also pray with the understanding" (vv. 14-15, italics mine).

When we pray in tongues, our spirits pray. We speak as the Holy Spirit (not our minds) gives us utterance. (See Acts 2:4.)

My wife and I and about a thousand other people witnessed a stirring example of this very phenomenon. It was 1987, and we were in a Network of Christian Ministers' meeting. Oral Roberts walked to the microphone and said, "I'm about to go on a ministry trip to Africa. Please pray for me." Suddenly, Brother Roberts stopped speaking to us in English and began to pray earnestly in a strange-sounding dialect.

Bud Sickler, a veteran missionary who ministers in Mombasi, Kenya, suddenly stood and walked to the platform. (Now Bud oversees scores of African churches, and he's no flake.) Sobbing brokenly, he said, "Brother

Roberts, I didn't know you spoke Swahili."

Obviously puzzled, Brother Roberts replied, "I don't know a word of Swahili. What do you mean? I was just praying out of my spirit."

"Brother Roberts," explained Bud, "it was a prayer of supernatural intercession. You were pleading, 'Give me the souls! Give me the souls of the Africans! Give me the souls!' "

That's a good example of how the Holy Spirit aids our intercession. You see, sometimes, we simply do not know what or how to pray. In intercession and spiritual warfare, we sometimes need additional divine empowerment and enablement. At those times, like the apostle Paul, we should say, "I will pray with the spirit," *not* "If I happen to feel like praying in tongues, I will pray with the spirit." We must learn to rely upon the wisdom and power of the Holy Spirit to help us intercede.

Remember Christ's promise to His disciples regarding the Holy Spirit? He said:

> And I will ask the Father, and He will give you another Comforter (Counselor, Helper, Intercessor, Advocate, Strengthener and Standby) that He may remain with you forever. The Spirit of Truth, Whom the world cannot receive (welcome, take to its heart), because it does not see Him, nor know and recognize Him. But you know and recognize Him, for He lives with you [constantly] and will be in you (John 14:16-17, Amplified).

That promise holds special meaning for Marcia Kendall, the head of Flame Fellowship, an organization that focuses on Spirit-led ministry to women. Marcia, a vivacious, capable woman, and her husband, John, who is an area director for the "700 Club," are dear friends of mine and members of my church.

In October 1985, John and Marcia were in Israel leading a Christian tour group of thirty-eight women and four men. Their group had traveled from Jordan to Israel and was on its way back to Jordan when their bus was unexpectedly stopped near the border. Before John and Marcia knew what was happening, the Arabs forced everyone in the tour group to relinquish all maps, books and belongings that were imprinted with the word "Israel."

Furious at this unwarranted intrusion, Marcia turned to their Muslim tour guide and demanded that he take her to the leader of these men. The guide, apprehensive about confronting the Arabs, cautioned John against such a move. But John, well-acquainted with his wife's courage and wisdom, instructed the man to take Marcia to the Arab commander.

As Marcia and the guide stepped off the bus and walked toward the military-looking barracks, the tour group prayed that God would protect Marcia and give her favor with the leader.

As Marcia entered the commander's makeshift office, she saw the items taken from her tour group piled high on the desk. Discovering that the Arab leader spoke English, Marcia said firmly, "We want our belongings returned to us."

At that point, the guide entered the conversation. Although both men spoke English, the pair ignored Marcia and began speaking in a language unknown to her. Indignant at such rude behavior, Marcia decided that she could play their game. If they want to speak in a foreign language in front of me, I'll speak in a foreign language, too, she reasoned silently. After all, I pray in tongues, don't I? So Marcia began to speak in tongues as the Holy

Spirit within her gave her utterance.

Keeping her eyes open and being careful not to raise the level of her voice above theirs, she held her chin high and prayed in the Spirit. The negotiations continued. From time to time, the men would ask Marcia a question in English, and she would answer in English.

In one such exchange, totally unaware that "Look into my eyes" was a phrase the Arabs frequently used as an expression of utmost sincerity, Marcia obeyed a strong impression from the Holy Spirit to stare straight at the commander and say in English, "*Look into my eyes* and tell me if I've come here to hurt your people."

As the Arab leader and guide continued their negotiations in their foreign language, Marcia continued praying confidently in tongues. Finally, the Arab leader picked up everything on his desk except one map and thrust the items into Marcia's arms. Triumphantly, Marcia and the tour guide made their way back to the bus.

Marcia couldn't believe her ears when the guide, obviously relieved that the ordeal was over and beaming from ear to ear, picked up the microphone on the bus and announced: "I know why you have let this woman be your leader. You should have heard her pleading your case *in Arabic* like one of our *lawyers*!"

Marcia didn't know Arabic. She didn't even realize that she was speaking Arabic. But the Holy Spirit knew Arabic, and He became Marcia's advocate, her counsel for the defense.

With Marcia Kendall's unique experience in mind, take a moment to ponder the breadth of meaning in the name "Comforter" (*parakletos*), which Jesus used in reference to the Holy Spirit. In his *Expository Dictionary of the New Testament Words*, W.E. Vine explains that the word means "called to one's side" and suggests the capability

106

or adaptability for giving aid. It was used in a court of justice to denote a legal assistant, a counsel for the defense, an intercessor or advocate who pleads another's cause.

Paul expands this thought in his letter to the believers at Rome:

> So too the (Holy) Spirit comes to our aid and bears us up in our weakness; for we do not know what prayer to offer nor how to offer it worthily as we ought, but the Spirit Himself goes to meet our supplication and pleads in our behalf with unspeakable yearnings and groanings too deep for utterance.
>
> And He Who searches the hearts of men knows what is in the mind of the (Holy) Spirit—what His intent is—because the Spirit intercedes and pleads [before God] in behalf of the saints according to and in harmony with God's will (Rom. 8:26-27, Amplified).

Are there ever times in prayer when you could use an advocate, an intercessor, to plead on your behalf? If so, remember that He has already been called alongside to help you. He resides within your spirit. Learn to yield your mouth and heart to Him. Learn to speak as He gives you the utterance. Allow Him to plead through you with unspeakable yearnings and groanings, knowing that He asks for nothing that is not in harmony with the perfect will of God.

Refuse to allow your proud intellect to intimidate or silence your spirit as the Holy Spirit prays through you. There will be many other times when you will pray with your mind, but some spiritual battles are won only by joining spirit with Spirit.

When your spirit feels weighted down and you have a heavy heart, don't say to yourself, I guess I'm just depressed. Realize that the all-wise, all-knowing Spirit of God may be nudging your spirit, trying to get your attention. Perhaps some person, some situation, needs your prayers. Instead of sinking into depression when that sensation of heaviness hits you, pray in your prayer language. The Holy Spirit needs a yielded vessel through which to intercede. Let Him use you!

Jesus Is Glorified

Do you long to glorify Jesus more and more, better and better? If so, then you will be especially interested in this fourth benefit of praying in tongues. Jesus said, "When He, the Spirit of truth, has come...*He will glorify Me*" (John 16:13-14, italics added). The Holy Spirit abiding within you enables you to glorify Jesus.

Have you ever become caught in praise and worship to God and simply "run out" of words in English? Has your natural vocabulary ever seemed too limited and restricted to express your adoration and awe for your omniscient, omnipresent, omnipotent God? This is the time to release your prayer language to God, allowing the Holy Spirit to help you glorify and lift up Jesus and enthrone Him upon your praises.

The Holy Spirit knows how to glorify Jesus through your praises, your life, your home, your work and in all you undertake. Ask the Holy Spirit to help you glorify Jesus. There is nothing He would rather do.

In fact, sometimes the Holy Spirit inspires a believer to pray in a language unfamiliar to the believer but known to an unbeliever within earshot—to glorify Jesus and serve as a sign to that individual. (See 1 Cor. 14:22.) I witnessed such a supernatural occurrence early in my Christian life.

Jerry Howell, a former hippie and drug addict whom I had led to the Lord, and I were students at Dallas Baptist University during the "Jesus Movement." Within ten months after Jerry gave his heart to the Lord, a thousand young people had been saved in our hometown of Kilgore, Texas. On weekends, Jerry and I would go home to Kilgore and minister in the various Christian coffee houses that had sprung up.

I was preaching that Jesus Christ was the same yesterday, today and forever, but the gifts of the Spirit were not released in my life, and I didn't have any real power in the Spirit. As a matter of fact, I didn't really believe in all that. It went against the grain of my religious tradition.

One night I was witnessing in Our House, a coffee house where Kilgore teenagers gathered every night for Bible study and prayer. A boy from India was there, and I was trying to lead him to the Lord.

As we walked by the prayer room, we overheard a person inside, praying in tongues. The guy from India stopped absolutely still and asked some bystanders, "What's that man doing in there?" Seeing that the boy had lost interest in our conversation, I left him with the other Christians and looked around for somebody else to minister to.

I lost track of the Indian boy that evening, but I later discovered what had happened to him. As we had walked by that prayer room, he had heard an American man speaking in Hindi, his native language. The man was exclaiming, "Lord Jesus, I magnify You. I praise You and love You." When the boy from India heard the American man glorifying and magnifying God in Hindi (a language the man praying had never learned), the boy was convicted of his sins and gave his heart to the Lord. After

I learned of his unique experience, the door of my heart began to open toward the Holy Spirit.

Remember my friends John and Marcia Kendall, whom I told you about earlier? This couple participated in a similar divine encounter arranged by the Holy Spirit to glorify Jesus and draw unbelievers closer to Him.

It was a Saturday morning in March 1971. John and Marcia were in New York on their way overseas with Gordon and Freda Lindsay, the founders of Christ for the Nations Institute in Dallas, Texas. Finding themselves in a strange city with time on their hands, John and Marcia decided to walk down the street and visit a synagogue. After all, they had always wanted to learn more about how Jesus Himself must have worshipped.

They had not gone to the synagogue with the idea of ministering to anyone or sharing about Jesus. They simply sat, reverently worshipping, feeling the presence of God. Simultaneously, they began to sing softly in tongues, magnifying the Lord, but being careful not to disturb any of the other worshippers.

When the service was over, a man seated in front of them turned around and said warmly, "Shalom! I see you're Jewish."

Supposing that the man had mistaken him for a Jew because of his black hair, John returned his greeting but explained that he was not Jewish.

"Where did you learn Hebrew? At the university?" the man asked.

Undaunted by John's reply that they didn't know Hebrew, the man invited John and Marcia to accompany him and several Jewish friends to a nearby restaurant for breakfast—which turned out to be lox, bagels and a shot of whiskey!

During breakfast, their host turned to John and said,

"I overheard you singing in Hebrew. Would you sing for us?"

"We don't speak or understand the Hebrew language," John repeated. "It was *God* who gave us the song you heard."

When the men expressed their desire to hear such a song, Marcia, at John's encouragement, shot a silent prayer heavenward and by faith sang for about fifteen seconds in a language inspired by the Spirit.

The reaction was immediate. Overcome with awe, the men excitedly interpreted what Marcia had sung. "Jewish women don't speak in high Hebrew, but your wife just did. The priest speaks it when he enters the holy of holies once a year. Your wife's song lifted up Jesus and spoke of the coming of the Lord."

Their conversation continued a few more minutes, then it was time to go. As the group stood and exchanged farewells, one man remarked almost wistfully, "You're enough to make us want to change our religion!"

The Kendalls later discovered that their Jewish waiter that morning had been a Christian who had been interceding for these very men.

To believers who might be tempted to make speaking in tongues work similarly for them, Marcia adds a word of caution. "God has chosen me in this way at other times. But on the few, unique occasions that God has enabled me to speak before someone in a language that I did not know, I never *tried* to make it happen. It was divinely arranged and inspired. God is looking for someone who will be small and simple enough to allow Him to be big enough. He uses us. We don't use the Holy Spirit."

How wonderful to know that one of the benefits of speaking in tongues is that we are enabled to glorify Jesus,

111

in whatever way God Himself deems best.

Your Spirit Is Rested and Refreshed

A fifth result of praying in tongues is rest and refreshment for your spirit. Isaiah prophesied:

> For with stammering lips and another tongue
> He will speak to this people, to whom He said,
> "This is the rest with which You may cause the
> weary to rest," and, "This is the refreshing"
> (Is. 28:11,12).

If you want to experience God's deep rest and "refreshing," pray in the Spirit.

In the Gospel of John, Jesus declared:

> "He who believes in Me, as the Scripture has said,
> out of his heart will flow *rivers* of living water."
> But this He spoke concerning the Spirit, whom
> those believing in Him would receive (John
> 7:38-39, italics mine).

Have you ever longed to sit down beside a beautiful river, dangle your feet in its cool, rippling waters and let it soothe your tired soul? The psalmist, who experienced similar longings, wrote: "He leads me beside the still and restful waters. He refreshes and restores my life—my self" (Ps. 23:2-3, Amplified).

You have a restful, refreshing river of life flowing out of your heart. Learn to enjoy the river of the Spirit. Release your prayer language and allow the Spirit to refresh and restore you.

Your Faith Is Built Up

Take a moment to read Jude 20 and 21, and you will discover another benefit of praying in the Spirit:

> But you, beloved, build yourselves up [founded]

112

on your most holy faith—make progress, rise like
an edifice higher and higher—*praying* in the Holy
Spirit; guard and keep yourselves in the love of
God...(Amplified, italics mine).

Notice that Jude did not say that praying in the Spirit
gives you faith; he said that by praying in the Holy Spirit,
you build yourselves up on your faith.

In verse 20, the word "praying" means, "by means
of praying." How do you build yourself up on your faith,
rising higher and higher like a building under construc-
tion? By means of praying in the Holy Spirit. That is how
your faith grows and is strengthened.

Notice also verse 21: "Guard and keep yourselves in
the love of God." If I were to ask fifty Christians what
the two most important elements of Christianity are,
what do you think the majority would say? I suspect they
would reply, Faith and love. But how do we stay built
up, strong in faith? How do we keep ourselves established
in the love of God? Jude told us the answer: by means
of praying in the Holy Spirit.

When you need faith, but faith seems to have left you,
what should you do? First of all, don't panic. Pray in the
Spirit. You will draw forth a spirit of faith that will take
over your wavering, fearful spirit.

If your enemy is snarling right in your face and you
are tempted to explode in anger, what should you do?
Keep yourself in the love of God by stopping right then
and praying in the Spirit.

Think of it this way. Verses 20 and 21 of Jude are like
an Oreo cookie. You have faith on one side. You have
love on the other. And you have the good stuff—prayer
in the Spirit—in the middle that holds the two together!
Learn to release your prayer language in those trying
times when faith or love seems weak.

113

You Receive Direction

Paul said in 1 Corinthians 14:13-14: "Therefore let him who speaks in a tongue pray that he may interpret. For if I pray in a tongue, my spirit prays, but my understanding is unfruitful." One way to develop hearing ears is to learn how to interpret what the Spirit of God is saying or praying through you. Praying or speaking in tongues is actually a form of communication, so if you speak in an unknown tongue to edify the church, you should ask the Holy Spirit for the interpretation. (See also 1 Cor. 14:5.) When you pray in tongues for your own edification, you should also learn to ask, "Holy Spirit, who or what were we praying for? What were we saying?"

I agree with the late Harold Horton, author of the classic *The Gifts of the Spirit*, a book that was first introduced in England in 1934. Horton, who was healed and received the baptism in the Holy Spirit under the ministry of the renown evangelist Smith Wigglesworth, said:

> It is obviously not necessary that everything we utter in private in other tongues should be clear to our understanding; but in circumstances where an interpretation is necessary or desirable, God will give one, that the understanding might profit as well as the spirit.[1]

An interpretation of tongues uttered in private can make clear to the understanding of the speaker what has already been an edification of his spirit in other tongues. (See 1 Cor. 14:13-14.)

Moreover, when you lay hands upon someone and pray over him or her in tongues, don't just stop there. Ask the Holy Spirit to show you what you were praying and to give you a word for that person. Paul instructed:

"But now, brethren, if I come to you speaking with tongues, what shall I profit you unless I speak to you either by revelation, by knowledge, by prophesying, or by teaching?" (1 Cor. 14:6).

In that verse, the Greek word Paul used for "revelation" (*apokalupsis*) means "uncovering, unveiling, or expressing the mind of God." "Knowledge" (*gnosis*) means "seeking to know, inquiring, investigating, especially in spiritual truth." "Prophesying" (*propheteia*) means "speaking forth the mind and counsel of God." And "teaching" (*didache*) refers to the act of instructing.

After you pray in tongues over someone, get very quiet in your spirit. Perhaps the Holy Spirit will communicate a message to your spirit that you are to share with that person.

Such a message may come to you in several ways. It may take the form of a mental image or picture. On other occasions, the Spirit may give you only one or two words or a brief phrase that you are to repeat. At other times, He may give you a detailed message to share. Always be sensitive to the Holy Spirit and allow Him to speak through you by revelation, knowledge, prophesying or teaching so that the person's understanding will profit. The Holy Spirit wants to give direction and instruction.

Once you learn to release your prayer language fluently and effortlessly in intercession or in a message in tongues, seek to take your next step in the Spirit. Pray for understanding. Learn to interpret what you have spoken or to allow the omniscient God to plant seeds of faith, wisdom, revelation, knowledge, direction, and so forth, in your mind; allow Him to water them, producing a spiritual harvest for yourself and for others. Allow the Holy Spirit to take you, and those for whom you pray, into higher realms of wisdom, revelation and knowledge concerning the affairs of this life.

It's Your Decision

One man puckered up his face as if he were being forced to swallow a dose of terrible-tasting cough syrup and asked pitifully, "Dr. Lea, do I *have* to pray in tongues?"

I replied, "No, sir. You don't *have* to; you *get* to! But if you decide not to pray in the Spirit, the Lord will still love you as much as always. You just won't get to enjoy as much of Him."

Many Christians today are like the believers of Samaria. They had believed the gospel, they had been baptized in water in the name of Jesus, but they had not yet received the Holy Spirit. (See Acts 8:5-17.) May I ask you the question Paul asked some disciples at Ephesus: *"Have you received the Holy Ghost since ye believed?"* (Acts 19:2, KJV, italics mine).

A Final P.S.

Before I conclude this lesson I would like to give a few words of instruction to those who have never received their prayer language, but who earnestly want to begin praying in the Spirit, releasing the seven benefits we've talked about.

First, let me ask a few questions. Have you bowed your will to God in surrender and humility, asking Him to forgive your sins, to come into your heart and become the Lord of your life? You see, salvation is a person's first step toward God, bringing that one into a new spiritual life and reality in Jesus and the Holy Spirit. But God does not take possession. You must give Him possession. You must first ask Jesus to come into your heart and be your

Savior before He can become your baptizer in the Holy Spirit. If you have not taken that first step toward God, there's no better time than now.

Now how did you receive Jesus into your heart? By faith, right? You asked, and He came in. How are your material needs met? The Scriptures instruct believers to ask and receive by faith. How do you receive physical healing from God? By faith, right? You get the picture. Actually, we receive *everything* from God by faith, including our prayer language.

Jesus said: "If you then, being evil, know how to give good gifts to your children, how much more will your heavenly Father give the Holy Spirit to those who ask Him!" (Luke 11:13). If you want to receive the Holy Spirit, simply ask your heavenly Father for this precious gift and receive Him by faith. Then release your prayer language. Do not speak in English or in your natural language. After all, you are receiving a *new* language from God, and you can't speak in two languages at once.

Just speak out by faith. Your new language will not come from your mind; the Holy Spirit will give you utterance. The same Jesus who turned water into wine (John 2) will take your natural breath, prayers and praises and transform them into a divine, spiritual utterance.

Some people receive a fluent language all at once. Others, according to the measure of their faith, may receive only a few words or phrases at first. Whatever God gives you, speak it out. Why should He give you more until you use what He has already given you?

You will find that praying in a prayer language is similar to praying in a natural language in that you are free to stop and start at will. Don't be afraid that if you stop speaking, you will not be able to begin again. After all, Jesus sent the Holy Spirit to abide with you forever.

Don't be surprised if your own intellect or Satan and his powers attempt to question your new experience. Your mind has been accustomed to being in control, but now your being is lining up in proper order: spirit, soul and body. If your mind complains, "I can't understand what you're saying," just reply: "You're not supposed to understand what I'm saying. I'm not talking to you. I'm talking to God!"

As you become accustomed to releasing your prayer language fluently and effortlessly, ask the Holy Spirit to speak to your mind and tell you whom or what you are praying for. Then continue to stand in faith and agreement with the Holy Spirit until you receive the answer.

Remember: Receiving your prayer language is not your goal; receiving and releasing the fullness of the indwelling Holy Spirit is a gateway to a whole new life of communion with God and to the manifestation of His love and power.

As you pray in your prayer language every day, you will begin to experience the seven wonderful benefits of praying in the Spirit. Like Adam and Eve in the garden, you will walk and talk with God and enjoy deep, intimate communion with Him, spirit to Spirit. Your ears will be opened to hear, know and obey Christ's voice. You will develop hearing ears!

Summing It Up

In chapter 6, we studied seven benefits of praying in tongues. What are those benefits?

1. *Gifts and power are released in your life.* The gift of tongues leads you into dimensions of the Spirit that you will never know otherwise.

2. *Your spirit is edified.* When you speak in tongues, you build up or recharge your spirit, prompting spiritual

growth. The more you pray in tongues, the more you are edified.

3. *The Spirit's prayer language aids intercession.* Sometimes you do not know what or how to pray. Sometimes you also need additional divine empowerment and enablement. You must rely upon the wisdom and power of the Holy Spirit to help you intercede.

4. *Jesus is glorified.* When you "run out" of words in English and your natural vocabulary and human understanding seem too limited and restricted to express your adoration and awe for God and His goodness, release your prayer language and the Holy Spirit will help you glorify and lift up the Lord.

5. *Your spirit is rested and refreshed.* If you want to experience God's deep rest and refreshment, you must learn to release your cares to God, pray in the Spirit and let God's restful, refreshing river of life flow out of your innermost being.

6. *Your faith is built up.* Praying in the Spirit does not give you faith; rather *by means of* praying in the Spirit, you build yourself up on your most holy faith and guard and keep yourself in the love of God.

7. *You receive direction.* As you learn to release your prayer language fluently and effortlessly in intercession or in a message in tongues, pray for understanding. Learn to interpret what you have spoken. Allow God to plant seeds of revelation, knowledge, wisdom and so forth in your mind that will produce a spiritual harvest for yourself and for others.

Personal Growth Activity 6

1. Which of the seven benefits of praying in the Spirit seems to be your greatest need at the moment?

_____ Gifts and power   _____ Rest and refreshment
_____ Edification of your spirit   _____ Building up your faith
_____ Help in intercession   _____ Direction
_____ Glorifying Jesus

2. If you want to enjoy these seven benefits of praying in the Spirit, ask God to enable you to release your prayer language as never before.

SECTION FOUR

Opening the Door Through Through The Lord's Prayer

CHAPTER SEVEN

Talking to God

If the angel Gabriel happened to overhear you praying, which word would he choose to describe your prayer: a monotonous monologue or a dynamic dialogue?

In this chapter and the next, I want to focus upon two fundamental questions regarding prayer as a dialogue. First, how does God want us to talk to Him in prayer? Second, how can we learn to hear God speak back to us?

In Matthew 6:9-13, Jesus gave us a model prayer. He commanded:

> In this manner, therefore, pray:
> Our Father in heaven,
> Hallowed be Your name.
> Your kingdom come.
> Your will be done
> On earth as it is in heaven.
> Give us this day our daily bread.
> And forgive us our debts,
> As we forgive our debtors.
> And do not lead us into temptation,
> But deliver us from the evil one.
> For Yours is the kingdom and the power and the

glory forever. Amen.

Jesus actually said, "Pray in this manner." What might that mean for us?

Words Are Important

In Luke 11:1-4, almost two years after giving the teaching in Matthew 6, Jesus repeated the same prayer almost word for word when His disciples asked, "Lord, teach us to pray." Once again He commanded His disciples to pray in that certain manner, using those words. Jesus obviously meant what He said.

Most of us don't understand the importance of words. It's easy to spout out a lot of idle words that we don't really mean. But when Jesus said something, He meant it. When He said something twice, He emphasized the importance of those precise phrases.

If you've ever consulted an attorney regarding some written contract you signed, you found out in a hurry that words are important. Even though the other party in your agreement might insist that he or she no longer wants to comply with the terms of the contract, that person's signature, along with yours, makes the contract binding. No matter how the other party argues and protests, your lawyer will keep bringing him or her back to the written agreement with these words: "But the *contract* says...."

Words are important. They reveal intentions and purposes. They record promises. It is no coincidence that Jesus repeated the same prayer outline two years later when His disciples came to Him and asked, "Lord, teach us to pray."

The Lord's Prayer Covers Our Needs

Just before I was to speak in a chapel service at ORU, the Lord impressed these words on my spirit: "Tell them that if they pray as I taught them I will begin to meet all their needs." As I've studied the Lord's prayer and used it for many years as a daily prayer guide, I've become convinced that the prayer represents our basic needs. Let me show you what I mean, using the words of the Lord's prayer as found in the familiar King James Version of the Bible.

God's Presence: "Our Father which art in heaven, Hallowed be thy name."

If you've ever felt all alone, as if you were totally removed from God's presence and estranged from His promises, you know the tremendous need that your spirit has for God Himself. The need to have God's presence in your life is represented in the very first topic of the Lord's prayer.

By what means are we enabled to enter the presence of God? By the shed blood of Jesus and by praise. (See Heb. 10:19-22; Ps. 95:2; 100:4.) Therefore, as you enter into prayer, thank God for Jesus and the blood He shed for you on the cross. After all, if it weren't for Jesus, you could not call God "Father." (See Gal. 4:4-6.)

Christians sometimes take their privileges for granted—for example, the privilege of calling God "our Father." We often rattle off the familiar first words of the Lord's prayer, "Our Father which art in heaven," and never stop to realize what we are saying. But the concept of becoming God's child and being able to call Him "Father" is totally foreign to many sincere people seeking after God. Such was the case for Madame Bilquis Sheikh of Pakistan, who shares the story of her search for God in her book *I Dared to Call Him Father*.

Madame Sheikh, a beautiful, dark-skinned, black-haired woman with large, expressive eyes and regal bearing, was born into a conservative Muslim family. For 700 years her aristocratic ancestors had been revered as landowners belonging to Pakistan's privileged upper class. Madame Sheikh's former husband, General Khalid Sheikh, served as Pakistan's minister of interior.

Frustrated and restless in her search for spiritual reality through the Muslim religion, Bilquis Sheikh ordered her chauffeur, a Christian, to bring her a Bible. Although Pakistanis had recently been murdered for even appearing to persuade Muslims to turn Christian, the frightened man managed to secure a cheaply bound little Bible for his wealthy employer.

Later that day as Madame Sheikh casually flipped open the strange book that seemed so important to the Christians, her attention was mysteriously drawn to one particular passage:

> I will call that My people, which was not My people; and her beloved, which was not beloved. And it shall be, that in the place where it was said unto them, Ye are not My people, there shall they be called sons of the living God (Rom. 9:25-26, Phillips).

The words puzzled her; the Muslims' holy book, the Koran, states again and again that God has no children.

During the next few days, Madame Sheikh continued reading both the Bible and the Koran side by side, turning from one to the other. She felt drawn to the Koran because of the loyalty of a lifetime, and she delved into the Bible because of a strange inner hunger and excitement.

126

Within the next few days, her young grandson became ill, and she had to check him into a nearby Catholic hospital. When a petite, bespectacled nun, the doctor in charge of the entire hospital, asked Madame Sheikh what she was doing with a Bible, she replied honestly, "I am earnestly in search of God."

Near the end of her conversation with the nun, Madame Sheikh confided, "I'm confused about your faith. You seem to make God so—I don't know—*personal*!"

The nun's reply shot through Madame Sheikh's being like electricity. With tears streaming down her cheeks, she stared earnestly into Madame Sheikh's eyes and said very quietly, "Talk to God as if He were your *father*."

After her grandson was discharged from the hospital and they returned home, Madame Sheikh went to her bedroom, got on her knees and tried to call God "Father." But afraid that it might be sinful to try to bring the Great One down to her own level, she gave up in frustration.

Later that night, however, remembering how her own beloved father, who had held high posts in the Indian government, had never been too busy to put aside his work and devote his full attention to her questions or problems, she got out of bed, sank to her knees on the rug, looked up to heaven and in rich new understanding called God "my Father."

Madame Sheikh was not prepared for what happened next. "Suddenly," she recalls, "that room wasn't empty any more. *He* was there! I could sense His Presence. I could feel His hand laid gently on my head...He was so close that I found myself laying my head on His knees like a little girl sitting at her father's feet. For a long time I knelt there, sobbing quietly, floating in His love. I found myself talking with Him, apologizing for not having known Him before...."

After a while, she reached to the bedside table where she kept the Bible and the Koran side by side, picked up both books and lifted them, one in each hand. "I am confused, Father," she said. "Which, Father?" she asked. "Which one is Your book?"

Suddenly she heard a voice inside her being, a voice that spoke to her as clearly as if she were repeating words in her inner mind. "In which book do you meet Me as your Father?" the voice asked.

The Bible was His book; there was no more questioning in her mind.[1]

As you speak the first phrase of the Lord's prayer, "Our Father which art in heaven," don't take those words for granted. Thank God that, because of Christ's suffering and finished work on Calvary, you can call Him Father. Praise Him because He has promised to hear your prayers and has graciously invited you to approach His throne at any time.

Then hallow the name of God—setting it apart and honoring it in your praises—by acknowledging who your Father is and what He has already done in Jesus Christ.

Many believers do not realize that through eight Old Testament names compounded with *Jehovah*, God revealed different dimensions of His character and pointed to their fulfillment in the new covenant through the person and work of Jesus Christ. If you want to discover a new dimension of praise and worship, as you pray, "Our Father which art in heaven, Hallowed be thy name," meditate upon these names, one by one, praising God for who He is and for the corresponding benefits you enjoy in the new covenant.

Take time to look up and read the Scripture references

to God's wonderful names and to turn those verses into powerful faith declarations of who God is and what He has accomplished for His children by virtue of the blood of Jesus.

Thank God that His name is *Jehovah-tsidkenu*, "the Lord my righteousness" (Jer. 23:5-6; Rom. 5:17-19), and *Jehovah-m'kaddesh*, "the Lord who sanctifies" (Lev. 20:8; 1 Cor. 6:11). Praise God that He is *Jehovah-shalom*, "the Lord is peace" (Judg. 6:24; Col 1:20-22), and *Jehovah-shammah*, "the Lord is there" (Ezek. 48:35; 1 Cor. 3:16). Adore God your Father because He is *Jehovah-rophe*, "the Lord who heals" (Ex. 15:22-26; 1 Pet. 2:24), and *Jehovah-jireh*, "the Lord's provision shall be seen" (Gen. 22:14: Rom. 8:32). Thank God because He is *Jehovah-nissi*, "the Lord my banner" (Ex. 17:15; Is. 11:10; 1 Cor. 15:57), and *Jehovah-rohi*, "the Lord my shepherd" (Ps. 23; Heb. 13:20).

Through praise to God your Father for who He is and for His covenant promises fulfilled in the person and work of Jesus Christ, you enter into the very presence of God, opening the way to bring your petitions before Him.

God's Priorities: "Thy kingdom come. Thy will be done in earth, as it is in heaven."

A second basic need you have is the need to experience the priorities of the kingdom ruling over yourself, your family, your church and your nation.

God reigns over you when you obey Him and accept His will and authority in your life. Therefore, at this second topic, declare that God's kingdom (His righteousness, joy and peace—Rom. 14:17) shall come and that His will and priorities shall be established in these four areas: 1. yourself; 2. your loved ones; 3. your church; 4. your nation.

Pray over each of these four areas, one by one, making this faith declaration: "Nobody is going to rule here but Jesus!" As you do this, declare kingdom order, kingdom power and kingdom priorities.

God's Provision: "Give us this day our daily bread."

Would you agree that a third basic need is the need to experience God's provision for your physical and material needs? Then I have good news for you: Jesus is the need-meeter, and He told us to pray daily, asking Him to supply our needs.

Because Jesus exhorted us in Matthew 6:33, "But seek first the kingdom of God and His righteousness, and all these things shall be added to you," I always pray over the needs of God's house, the church, before I pray over the needs of my own house. I challenge you to do that, too.

I don't pray over my needs in generalities; instead, as best as I know how, I tell the Lord specifically what I need, just as Paul instructed believers to do: "Do not fret or have any anxiety about anything, but in every circumstance and in everything by prayer and petition [definite requests] with thanksgiving continue to make your wants known to God" (Phil. 4:6, Amplified).

Don't get me wrong. If you need shoes, I'm not saying that you always have to say, "God, please send me a pair of black, wing-tip, size 11-1/2, AA width, Florsheim shoes." If God knows the number of hairs on your head, I'm sure He knows your shoe size. Tell God your needs, then allow Him the privilege of doing "superabundantly, far over and above all that we [dare] ask or think— infinitely beyond our highest prayers, desires, thoughts, hopes or dreams." (See Eph. 3:20, Amplified.)

On the other hand, the Holy Spirit sometimes inspires us to pray very specifically so our own faith might be built up and so God might be glorified.

Tucked away in the prolific writings of the beloved, retired radio evangelist C.M. Ward is a true story that illustrates beautifully this scriptural principle of praying specifically and making definite requests. Ward records the miraculous occasion when Assemblies of God missionaries Kenneth Ware and his wife, a French Jewess, proved the practicality of this principle.

The time was September 1944. The place was 22 rue Ruchonnet, Lausanne, Switzerland. Because they had hidden Jews from the Nazis and cooperated with the French resistance, the Wares and their infant son had been forced to leave France and take up residence in Switzerland.

On this particular Saturday morning when Mrs. Ware came to her husband and asked him for shopping money, he said he didn't have a single penny to give her. A few minutes later, Brother Ware heard his wife praying, speaking to her Lord in utter simplicity:

"Jesus, I need five pounds of potatoes, two pounds of pastry flour, apples, pears, a cauliflower, carrots, veal cutlets for Saturday and beef for Sunday." He even heard his wife tell God the brand of flour she preferred. After Mrs. Ware had listed her requests she said, "Thank You, Jesus." Then she began to prepare breakfast.

At 11:30 that same morning, Mrs. Ware answered a knock at their apartment door. There stood a radiant-faced, blue-eyed blond man wearing the customary long blue apron of a deliveryman. "Mrs. Ware," he said in perfect French without the customary Swiss accent, "I am bringing you what you asked for."

"There must be a mistake," Mrs. Ware protested as the man made his way to her kitchen. "I have not asked for anything."

Certain that the stranger had knocked on their door

by mistake, Brother Ware sided with his wife. "Sir," he said, "there are twenty-five apartments in this building, and you are surely making some mistake."

But the man's reply was as firm as before. "Mrs. Ware," he said in a low, sweet voice, "I am bringing what *you* asked for." Then he emptied the grocery basket, placing on the table *the exact items*—no more, no less—that Mrs. Ware had talked to God about before breakfast that morning. The two pounds of pastry flour were the very brand she had requested.

Brother Ware turned to apologize because he didn't have money to tip the man, but the stranger's look of reproach sealed his lips. Mrs. Ware accompanied the smiling deliveryman to the door, and Brother Ware walked to the window to watch as the man left the building. But they were overcome with awe at what happened next.

"There was only one way for him to pass, and that was before the window where I was standing," recalls Brother Ware. "But though I watched and Mrs. Ware opened the door again to examine the hallway, he was gone. There was no trace of him anywhere!"[2]

Is that miraculous event hard to believe? Perhaps we need to read again the apostle's injunction to the Philippian believers: "Do not fret or have any anxiety about anything, but in every circumstance and in everything by prayer and petition [definite requests] with thanksgiving continue to make your wants known to God."

One day as I was taking a walk and communing with God, I heard His familiar voice in my spirit: "Do you want to know why I bless you so? Because you believe I will."

When you face a need, refuse to allow discouragement or unbelief to rob you. Instead, continue to pray daily over that need, voicing specific, definite requests, until you receive your answer.

Getting Along With People: "And forgive us our debts, as we forgive our debtors."

We all have the need to experience forgiveness from God for our sins and shortcomings, and we also need to forgive others for their sins against us.

I often have the need to say, "Lord, forgive me for my bad attitude," or "Forgive me for that harsh word." Every time I ask God's forgiveness, the Holy Spirit always says, "Forgiven!" He never condemns; He never holds my failure over my head. He deals the same way with you. We must respond to the sins of others against us in that same loving way. By exercising love and forgiveness, we can learn to get along with others. People may not desire to get along with us all the time, but we can certainly do our part to get along with them.

On the cross, even as His enemies were slandering, torturing and crucifying Him, Jesus was getting along with them. What do I mean by that? He was responding to them in love. He was praying for His enemies: "Father, forgive them, for they do not know what they do" (Luke 23:34).

Bitterness and unforgiveness are emotions you dare not hide away in your heart; like powerful acids, they will gradually erode and destroy the very vessel that contains them. Therefore, as you are praying each day, learn to forgive those who have offended you and set your will that you will "be kind to one another, tenderhearted, forgiving one another, just as God in Christ also forgave you" (Eph. 4:32).

Power Over the Devil: "And lead us not into temptation, but deliver us from evil."

You need continual deliverance from temptation and

from the powers of Satan that are trying to pull you off track. At the beginning of every day, pray a hedge of protection about yourself, your loved ones and your possessions. (See Ps. 91:9-11; Job 1:9-10, Amplified.)

Some may protest, "Is it really important to pray every day and commit myself, my loved ones and my possessions into the hands of God?" I'll let you read a story that the late Gordon Lindsay, founder of Christ for the Nations Institute and a mighty intercessor, shared in his book *Prayer That Moves Mountains*, and *you* determine the answer to that question. Lindsay writes:

> The importance of daily prayer, a daily meeting with God, and not just a casual saying of prayers is forcefully illustrated in the story of a Christian Armenian merchant who was carrying merchandise by caravan across the desert to a town in Turkish Armenia. Having been brought up by Christian parents he had formed a life habit of daily committing himself into the hands of God.
>
> At the time of this incident, the country was infested with "Kurds," that is, bandits who lived by robbing caravans. Unknown to the merchant, a band of these highwaymen had been following the caravan, intending to rob it at the first camping place on the plains.
>
> At the chosen hour, under cover of darkness, they drew near. All was strangely quiet. There seemed to be no guards, no watchers but, as they pressed up, to their astonishment, they found high walls where walls had never stood before.
>
> They continued to follow, but the next night they found the same impassable walls. The third night the walls stood, but there were breaches in them through which they went in.

The captain of the robbers, terrified by the mystery, awakened the merchant.

"What does this mean?" said he. "Ever since you left Ezerum, we have followed, intending to rob you. The first night and the second night we found high walls around the caravan but, tonight, we entered through broken places. If you will tell us the secret of all this, I will not molest you."

The merchant himself was surprised and puzzled. "My friends," he said, "I have done nothing to have walls raised about us. All I do is pray every evening, committing myself and those with me to God. I fully trust in Him to keep me from all evil; but tonight, being very tired and sleepy, I made a rather half-hearted lip prayer. That must be why you were allowed to break through!"

The Kurds were overcome by such testimony as this.

Then and there, they gave themselves to Jesus Christ and were saved. From caravan robbers, they became God-fearing men. The Armenian, however, never forgot that breach in the wall of prayer.[3]

When we pray and walk in obedience to the Word, we defeat the spiritual forces of the enemy. By consistent, earnest prayer, the enemy is held at bay and God's hedge of protection is maintained about us.

In addition to praying for a hedge of protection, you should also put on the whole armor of God as outlined in Ephesians 6:14-18, by believing and declaring who Jesus, your armor of light, is (see Rom. 13:12,14). Fully clad in the armor of God and encircled by God's hedge of protection, you can stand secure in the victory Jesus has won for you.

A Divine Partnership: "For thine is the kingdom, and the power, and the glory, for ever. Amen."

You need to be a participant in God's kingdom, His power and His glory. Praise God because He is delivering you from every evil work and preserving you for His heavenly kingdom. (See 2 Tim. 4:18; Luke 12:32.) Thank God that He has given you the authority to trample on serpents and scorpions and over all the *power* of the enemy. (See Luke 10:19.) Give Him praise because you are being transformed into the image of Christ, from *glory to glory*, by the Spirit of the Lord. (See 2 Cor. 3:18; Heb. 2:9-10.) Thank God because He has made you a participant in His kingdom, power and glory.

Now do you understand why I say that the model prayer Christ gave us covers every basic need of your life? God has abundantly provided for your needs for His presence, priorities and provision. He has taught you how to get along with people, how to overcome the power of Satan and how to be a participant in His kingdom, power and glory. Therefore, each day you should leave your place of prayer walking in continual thanksgiving and praise.

We have studied how to take the beautifully balanced model prayer that Jesus has given us and use it to talk to God, but just talking to God is not enough. We also need to hear what God is saying back to us as we dialogue and commune with Him. We need to know what to do with the creative, transforming words we hear. That's exactly what my next chapter is all about.

Summing It Up

Each of the six topics in the Lord's prayer not only represents a basic human need, but also serves as an open line of communication with God for the meeting of that need.

God has abundantly provided for all your needs for His presence, priorities and provision. He has taught you how to get along with people, how to overcome the power of Satan and how to be a participant in His kingdom, power and glory. Therefore, each day you should leave your place of prayer walking in continual thanksgiving and praise.

Personal Growth Activity 7

1. Of the six topics in the Lord's prayer, which represents the greatest need in your life at the moment?

   _____ God's presence: "Our Father which art in heaven, Hallowed be thy name."

   _____ God's priorities: "Thy kingdom come. Thy will be done in earth, as it is in heaven."

   _____ God's provision: "Give us this day our daily bread."

   _____ Getting along with people: "And forgive us our debts, as we forgive our debtors."

   _____ Power over the devil: "And lead us not into temptation, but deliver us from evil."

   _____ Divine partnership: "For thine is the kingdom, and the power, and the glory, for ever. Amen."

2. What is the strongest desire welling up within your heart right now regarding the truths presented in this lesson?

   _____

   _____

   _____

   _____

   _____

   _____

   _____

   _____

   _____

   _____

   _____

   _____

CHAPTER EIGHT

Hearing God Speak

We've seen that the six topics of the Lord's prayer help us express our most basic needs to God, but they also do more. These words serve as powerful declarations which, when prayed in faith, open the door into the supernatural realm of communion with God.

Entering the Presence and Power of God

I don't know much about computers, but this book was typed on a word processor. Each chapter was given a code name under which it was stored in the computer's memory. Later, if someone wanted to bring a chapter up on the screen of the computer, that person had to type in the proper code name and ask the computer to retrieve and display the chapter. In other words, if the individual wanted to get into the memory of the computer, he or she had to use the correct code and follow the proper procedure.

I don't want to carry such a simplistic analogy too far, but I'd like you to think of each topic in the Lord's prayer as a "code name" that grants you entrance into the presence and power of God in reference to that particular area of need. Jesus said, "When you pray, say...," and He gave us a powerful prayer outline that, if followed under the guidance of the Holy Spirit, takes us right into the holy presence of God.

Transforming Prayer

Once you have entered God's gates with thanksgiving and come into His courts with praise, once you have opened the door into the supernatural realm of communion with God, what do you do next?

Actually, I have discovered four steps for believers to take if they want their prayers to be transformed from boring monologues into dynamic dialogues. Here are those four steps.

Pray Until You Feel a Release

Pray over each topic in the Lord's prayer until you feel a release in your spirit. Once you have prayed over a topic, saying all that you feel needs to be said, your spirit will "relax," knowing that your prayers or praises have been released to God.

Beware of a common mistake. Feeling their spirits relax inside, many believers do one of two things. They either stop praying, get up and go about their business, or they think of the next topic they want to pray about and immediately talk to God about it. Don't do that. Instead, when you feel your spirit relax, just pause and get quiet inside.

Expect a Response

You have talked to God; now wait and see if He wants to talk to you. If you have released your prayer or petition to God and opened your ears to hear His voice, what comes up and through your spirit may be God's answer for that need in your life. He may say only a word or two. He may give you an idea, a verse of Scripture or a revelation. But if you want to hear Him, you must learn to be quiet and wait in God's presence once your prayer has been released to Him. At that point, expect to hear God speak back to your spirit.

In his insightful book *Is That Really You, God?*, a virtual textbook in the art of hearing God, Loren Cunningham, founder and director of Youth With a Mission, tells how his godly, praying parents taught him to expect a response when he talked to the Lord.

It was almost dinner time one evening when nine-year-old Loren came wandering into the kitchen where his mom was preparing cornbread and red beans for supper. "Loren," she said, "We're out of milk. Can you go over to the widow's store and buy some?" Handing him a $5 bill, she cautioned, "Now be careful with this. That's our grocery money for the week."

Loren stuck the bill into the pocket of his jeans, whistled for his dog and headed for the store. But, typical boy that he was, on his way he also kicked a can along, stopped to investigate a bottle cap or two and picked up a stick to clatter down the neighbor's fence.

You guessed it. At the store, he reached into his pocket to pay for the milk, and the money was gone.

Panic stricken, Loren ran back the way he had come, searching frantically everywhere he had stopped. But it was no use. There was nothing to do but go home and tell his mother that he had lost her money.

His mother's face darkened when Loren admitted what he had done. It was a large loss. Then she quickly brightened.

"Come, son, let's pray," she said. "We'll ask God to show us where the money is."

Putting her hand on Loren's slender shoulder, his

mother began to talk to God. "Lord, You know exactly where that $5 bill is hiding. Now we ask You to show us. Speak to our minds, please, for You know that we need that money to feed the family."

Loren watched as his mother stood there, her eyes shut. Suddenly his mother's grip tightened on his shoulder. "Loren," she said, "God just told me the money is under a bush." Then she quickly darted out the door, and Loren scrambled to catch up.

It was almost dusk as they retraced Loren's path to the store, inspecting every hedge and bush. It was nearly too dark to see by the time his mother stopped, looking down the street toward a certain thick evergreen shrub. "Let's try that one!" she said, heading straight for the bush. The two peered underneath and there, way back at the base of the stubby trunk, was the $5 bill.

Sipping tall glasses of milk with their beans and cornbread that night, Loren's family rejoiced at how God cared for them that day.[1]

You may not always need a specific reply to your prayer such as Loren and his mother received. But, as God's sheep, you can expect to hear your shepherd's voice whenever He desires to give you a word of comfort, counsel or instruction. Just get quiet and allow God to speak back to your spirit.

Write Down What You Hear

Ask God to give you ears that hear His voice; then when He speaks, write down His creative words to you. Keep a notebook or a copy of my *Could You Not Tarry One Hour? Prayer Diary* nearby and record what the Lord speaks to your heart as you pray. When the Spirit of God flashes a revelation, Scripture verse or command into your spirit, write it down and then continue praying. Treasure God's words to you. Declare them out loud.

God may speak to you about your children. He may give you a word of wisdom or knowledge. He may talk to you about your job. He may direct you to an open door of opportunity or ministry. On the other hand, if you don't hear anything, just be patient. As you train and develop your spiritual hearing, you will begin to hear God.

As Romans 10:17 says, "So then faith comes by hearing, and hearing by the word of God." "Word" here is the Greek word *rhema*, meaning God's spoken statement, command or instruction for a particular situation. When God speaks, write down the *rhema* word that the Lord gives you and meditate upon it to build your faith.

Ephesians 6:17 says, "And take...the sword of the Spirit, which is the word of God." Once again, "word," as used here, is *rhema*. Write down God's words to you and use them as a sharp sword to drive back the enemy and defeat him.

As you sense that God has finished speaking to you on that particular prayer topic, go on to the next topic and repeat the steps we have just talked about.

Praise God That You Are Beginning to Hear

Once you begin hearing from God when you pray, you won't be bored or depressed when you leave your daily place of prayer. No matter what the outward circumstances of your life, you will be walking and talking in victory because you will have received God's *rhema* word on the matter.

Many individuals who have been Christians for years would have to confess that, to their knowledge, they have never received a *rhema* word from God. Others, not realizing that they can hear God for themselves, have made a practice of running to someone who has a reputation for hearing the voice of the Lord whenever an emergency arises.

But obedient believers—who have expanded their time of fellowship with the Lord and learned to discern what is or is not in keeping with His Word, His will and His character—have every right to expect to hear from God directly in matters that pertain to them or to their loved ones.

In his book *Is That Really You, God?* Loren Cunningham also shares how his godly mother taught him a valuable lesson along this very line.

One February morning three months after the experience with the lost grocery money, Loren's father announced that, for a few days, he was going to have to be away from home and the sixty-member church he pastored. Since he would be journeying halfway across the country to Springfield, Missouri, Loren's father gave his ten-year-old son instructions to take care of the family while he was gone.

But Loren and his mother were totally unprepared for the phone call that came a few days later. The voice on the other end of the line informed them that Brother Cunningham had been stricken with appendicitis and that an operation was impossible. To make matters even worse, due to wartime shortages, there was no penicillin. Therefore, the voice continued, it was just a matter of time until he would die.

Loren's mother hung up the phone and announced that they needed to pray—hard! Loren crawled behind the couch and stayed there for hours, praying his heart out.

Two days passed, and Loren's father continued about the same. Loren recalls, "We had to hear something from God—some word to help us hold on." Then an event took place which Loren would never forget.

Three days after they learned of Cunningham's attack,

someone knocked on the door. Loren watched as his mother opened it. There, looking even more sober than usual and acting as if he were afraid to speak what was on his mind, stood a man from their church.

"What is it?" asked Loren's mother.

"Sister Cunningham," the man blurted, "God gave me a dream of your husband coming home in a coffin."

Loren anxiously scanned his mother's face as she stood there silent, deep in thought. Then she spoke.

"Well, sir," she said kindly, but firmly, "I do appreciate your coming here to tell me this. Hard as it is, I promise I will ask God if the dream really is from Him. With something this important, He'll tell me Himself, won't He?"

Loren recalls, "It was more of a statement than a question. With that, Mom thanked the gentleman a second time and held open the door. Then she went to prayer.

" 'Is that You, God?' she asked. 'I promise to try to accept this man's words if they are really from You. Just let me know, that's all I ask.' "

Says Loren, "Mother had such a believing relationship with her heavenly Father that she fully expected Him to answer her on such an important issue in a fatherly-type manner, with no shadow of doubt. She left it with God and went to bed."

The next morning as the children sat down to their breakfast of steaming oatmeal, their mother announced that she had some good news. "I had a dream last night," she said. "In my dream Dad came home, but it was on a train, and he was wearing his pajamas!"

"And that's exactly what happened," remembers Loren. "We received word that Dad had recovered enough to want to return to California. He had trouble making travel arrangements because of the wartime military priorities, but through friends, he managed to get a berth on a Pullman sleeping car. So Dad arrived just as Mom had known he would, on a train, wearing his pajamas. We must have been a sight, walking down the station platform, supporting our still weak, shaky father who shuffled along in his bedroom slippers. But Dad didn't care. Neither did we. He was home."

Later, as the family rejoiced together over Brother Cunningham's miraculous recovery and thanked God for the word of knowledge He had given Loren's mother, she pointed out an important aspect of guidance. "Getting God's leading for someone else is tricky," she said. "We can hear a confirming voice through another person. But if God has something important to tell you, He will speak to you directly."[2]

Don't misunderstand my point in sharing this wonderful story with you. I am not saying that believers should be unteachable or that we shouldn't seek counsel. Neither am I saying that God does not sometimes speak to us through someone else. On the other hand, God is also perfectly capable of speaking directly to you. Learn to submit to Him the counsel or words you receive from others. He will confirm whether or not the message is from Him.

In those inevitable times of emergency when you, like Loren and his mother, must have a clear, unshakable, *rhema* word from God to anchor your faith to, you will be glad that you have taken the time to sit in God's presence, listening to His voice. You will praise God that you have developed big, discerning, spiritual ears.

Consistent, heartfelt communication with God is essential if prayer is to become a supernatural dialogue instead of a monotonous monologue. As your relationship and communication with God deepen, the impossible will become possible in your life, your family, your business. You will walk in hope and confidence because God, the life and power-source of the universe, is guiding your steps, seeing your needs beforehand and making divine provision for them.

Summing It Up

In the familiar topics of the Lord's prayer, Jesus has given a powerful prayer outline that, if followed under the guidance and anointing of the Holy Spirit, takes you directly into the presence of God.

As you learn to take four basic steps in prayer, you will develop hearing ears. First, as you pray over each topic of the Lord's prayer, wait until your spirit releases all its praises or petitions to God and "relaxes." Second, when you sense that release in your spirit, get very still before God and expect to hear a response from Him. Third, write down what you hear. And, finally, don't forget to praise God that you are beginning to hear His voice in prayer.

Your prayer monologues will turn into dialogues with God.

Personal Growth Activity 8

1. Which of the steps to hearing God in prayer came as "new information" for you?

    _____ Pray over each topic in the Lord's prayer until your spirit "relaxes."

    _____ Expect a response.

    _____ Write down what you hear.

    _____ Praise God that you are beginning to hear.

2. Do you already have a prayer diary or journal?

    _____ Yes   _____ No

3. If you own such a journal, do you use it consistently?
   _____ Yes   _____ No

4. Complete the following sentence:
   In this chapter this point challenged my heart more than any other
   truth presented: _____
   _____
   _____
   _____
   _____
   _____
   _____
   _____

SECTION FIVE

Learning to Obey

CHAPTER NINE

Hearing and Obedience

Kathryn Kuhlman once said, "If you're going to be led by the Holy Spirit, you have to be willing to follow." You see, it's not enough to hear God; we must also obey what He says, for along with hearing come responsibility and accountability.

You and I are responsible and accountable for what we hear. That is why I believe this final chapter dealing with hearing and obedience could very well contain the most vital, practical teaching in the entire book.

The Importance of Obeying God's Voice

Why is obedience of such critical importance? I can think of at least four good reasons.

God Judges Those Who Refuse to Hear

You and I live in a day when many people—Christians and sinners alike—don't like to talk about judgment. "God is a God of love," they protest. "Judgment and punishment aren't compatible with God's nature and character." I've got news for those people. They'd better read the Bible and wise up.

Sure God is a God of love. Who said He isn't? But if you want a glimpse into the great heart of God, read the words a grief-stricken God spoke to Jeremiah when the people He loved refused to hear His words and went whoring after other gods. Can you hear the sorrow in God's voice as He says, "I have cast off My heritage; I have given *the dearly beloved of My life* into the hand of her enemies" (Jer. 12:7, Amplified, italics mine)?

Have you, like God, ever had to release and say good-bye to the dearly beloved of your life: someone you loved, but who no longer loved you? If so, you know how a brokenhearted God must have felt as He watched the people of Israel turn a deaf ear to His pleadings and stride belligerently down a road toward destruction:

> Hear and give ear:
> Do not be proud,
> For the Lord has spoken.
> Give glory to the Lord your God
> Before he causes darkness,
> And before your feet stumble
> On the dark mountains....
> But if you will not hear it,
> My soul will weep in secret for your pride;
> My eyes will weep bitterly
> And run down with tears,
> Because the Lord's flock has been taken
> captive (Jer. 13:15-17).

Don't ever think that God won't let you go your own way. He will cry bitter tears over the misery and bondage brought on by your own sins and for the judgment waiting for you around the corner. He will weep in secret for your pride. But if you spurn His love and stubbornly refuse to part with your rebellious ways, He will help you pack your bags and walk you to the door. And when you're out of earshot, He'll weep over you and the tragic lessons you're about to learn—the hard way.

God Is Faithful to the Repentant

God is not only faithful to judge sin; He is also faithful to restore the repentant. If you, like Jeremiah's countrymen, have turned a deaf ear to God's word to you in the past, if you have brought sorrow and judgment upon yourself, repent and turn to God, and you will experience His mercy and restoration. Keep your ears turned to His voice and He will speak to you again.

In the Book of Lamentations, Jeremiah bewailed Jerusalem's destruction at the time of the Babylonian captivity. God's people had become so corrupt that Jehovah had forsaken His sanctuary and abandoned it to enemies. Yet Jeremiah declared:

> Through the Lord's mercies we are not consumed,
> Because His compassions fail not.
> They are new every morning;
> Great is Your faithfulness (Lam. 3:22-23).

I've got news for you. God hasn't run out of mercy. Even if we have ignored or disobeyed His voice in the past, we can count on His faithfulness and mercy if we will repent and obey.

Success Is Dependent Upon Hearing and Obeying

There's a third reason why obedience is so important. In Matthew 7:24-27 Jesus likened success or failure in the kingdom of God to one thing—hearing and obedience:

> Therefore whoever *hears these sayings of Mine,
> and does them*, I will liken him to a wise man
> who built his house on the rock; and the rain

153

descended, the floods came, and the winds blew and beat on that house; and it did not fall, for it was founded on the rock.

Now everyone who *hears these sayings of Mine, and does not do them*, will be like a foolish man who built his house on the sand; and the rain descended, the floods came, and the winds blew and beat on that house; and it fell. And great was its fall'' (italics mine).

Success is sure if God's voice is heard and obeyed, but failure is certain if it is rejected.

Note this carefully. The only way you will be able to stand against the onslaughts coming in the dark days ahead is to begin now to hear and obey God's voice. Your ultimate success or failure is dependent upon learning to hear God's voice and obeying.

Refuse to let Satan and his demonic powers snatch the truth from your heart. Refuse to allow your own human desires and reasoning to twist and pervert the truth in order to make it conform to your personal wants and wishes. If you hear God's word to you and yet refuse to obey, it is only a matter of time until the restless waters of trouble and bitter winds of adversity bring your house tumbling down.

Obedience Births Blessing

Why is it important to obey God? Here's a fourth reason: A little obedience births a lot of blessing. This true story from my own life will help you understand what I mean by that statement.

Some time near the end of 1978 or the beginning of 1979—I don't remember exactly when—Frank and Ann Allen felt prompted to invite me to Rockwall, Texas, to lead a Bible study. They obeyed that impression. Frank called and asked if I'd meet him at a local restaurant—to talk.

During our meal, Frank put down his fork, leaned forward and said: "Larry, I don't know if this is really of the Lord or not, but I have had this impression that you are to lead a Bible study in my home. Why don't we do it for a time or two and see what it means?"

Later, Frank and Ann drove to Kilgore, Texas, where I was preaching a revival at Pastor B.J. Willhite's church, and we discussed the matter further. At that time, none of us had any inkling that it was a big deal. We were simply seeking to be obedient to the gentle nudgings of the Holy Spirit.

Some time after that, I felt prompted that I really was supposed to go to Rockwall for the Bible study we had discussed. If I'd been looking for some big opportunity to get on television or to make a name for myself, I wouldn't have pursued that prompting. But I was seeking to follow the leading of the Holy Spirit.

Several months later while I was holding a revival in Canada, the Spirit of God spoke to my heart and said, "Go to Rockwall and establish My people there." I had no idea what that meant, but I had come far enough in my spiritual development just to go ahead and obey God.

Out of those Bible studies and prayer meetings in the home of Frank and Ann Allen, Church on the Rock was birthed in January 1980. In less than seven years, our numbers grew from thirteen to more than 5,000 active members; we now have a thirty-four-member, full-time pastoral staff; more than 400 CARE (home cell) groups and an annual budget of $8 million. Why? Because a little obedience births a lot of blessing.

Has God been asking you to do something? Have you brushed it aside because it seemed unimportant? Don't expect further words from God until you obey what He has already told you to do. You may be surprised where that one little step of obedience takes you.

Over and over in the New Testament we find these words: "He who has an ear, let him hear...." Even in the last book of the Bible, Jesus repeated the warning: "He who has an ear, let him hear what the Spirit says to the churches..." (Rev. 2:7).

Did you notice that Jesus didn't say, "Hear what the Spirit *said* to the churches"? No, He said, "Hear what the Spirit *says* to the churches." Do you get it? The Spirit of God has not stopped speaking. His silence is not the problem. The problem is that *we* may not be listening. In the days ahead, the question is not going to be, "Did God speak?" The question will be, "Did you obey?"

Yes, God is speaking today. When He speaks to you, how should you respond?

How to Recognize and Obey God's Voice

Before we study the nine, practical steps I'm about to share with you, please allow me to emphasize that I do not run legalistically through every one of them in a certain order every time a voice speaks to me. I have listened to God's voice for so long now that if I have a question or uneasy feeling about something I have heard in my spirit, I usually know what steps to take.

These procedures are safe, scriptural requirements for every believer determined to develop hearing ears and to walk in the perfect will of God. Following these practical steps will help prevent many painful blunders and deadly mistakes.

Submit to Christ's Lordship

I'll bet it has happened to you. You have prayed and

heard a voice in your heart or an idea has popped into your mind. Or maybe somebody came to you with what he or she felt was a word from the Lord. But there was a problem. You weren't quite sure that the voice, idea or word was really from God. What should you do?

First of all, submit the issue totally to the lordship of Jesus Christ. As the Lord of your life, He knows how He wants to bless you, what He desires to develop in you, what He plans to do through your life. It's up to you to come to the place where your own desires concerning the matter are neutral, where you want nothing but His perfect will. Submit the idea or situation to the lordship of Jesus and ask for nothing more, nothing less, nothing else than the perfect will of God.

Don't be like the people of Israel who insisted on having their own way:

> ...They hastily forgot His works; they did not [earnestly] wait for His plans [to develop] respecting them; but lusted exceedingly in the wilderness, and tempted and tried to restrain God [with their insistent desire] in the desert. And He gave them their request, but sent leanness into their soul and [thinned their numbers by] disease and death (Ps. 106:13-15, Amplified).

Do you know what those verses say to me? They say you can be stubborn and rebellious and insist that God give you what you want. But in the end, you may not want what you get!

It's far better to submit the matter to Christ's lordship and let Him guide you in the way He knows is best.

Have Faith That God Will Speak to You

When you are born again, Someone who is righteous and holy, wise and good, strengthening and satisfying comes into your heart. He wants to teach you how to walk according to the Word of God and by His inner revelation. After you submit an issue to God and declare, "Thy kingdom come. Thy will be done," maintain a spirit of expectancy and faith. Commune with God and pray in the Spirit, lifting up the matter before Him. Be assured that God will not leave you dangling without direction. Have faith that He will not allow you to be led astray when you are earnestly desiring His will. Open your heart and spiritual ears and wait for His voice to speak by whatever means He desires.

Sometimes God reveals His will to you by an impression. Sometimes He speaks by an inner voice. Sometimes you can hear His voice speaking to you through the voice of someone or something else—a stranger, a friend, the words of a song, a thought from a book, a verse of Scripture.

Have you ever heard God speak directly to you? Does He speak in sentences? He does to me. The first time I heard God speak to me was when He saved me. He told me that I would be a minister to young people. It was almost three years before I heard His voice again. That time He said, "I love you." The impact of those words nearly knocked me out of my chair. Over the years as I began to "grow" my spiritual ears, I have heard Him speak more and more.

It bothers some Christians when they hear me say that God speaks to me. But do you know what bothers me? The fact that they aren't enjoying the privilege of hearing God speak to them.

Know that God wants to speak to you. After you have submitted to Christ's lordship, stop fretting and rest in Him, confident that His word to you is on its way. In His time, in His way, you will hear His voice.

Listen as God Transmits His Word Into Your Spirit

Sometimes the Holy Spirit speaks directly to your spirit, giving you "inside information" on what is going on or is about to happen. If that sounds like strange doctrine to you, check it out in John 16:13-14:

> But when He, the Spirit of Truth (the truth-giving Spirit) comes, He will guide you into all the truth—the whole, full truth. For He will not speak His own message—on His own authority—but He will tell whatever He hears [from the Father, He will give the message that has been given to Him] and He will announce and declare to you the things that are to come—that will happen in the future. He will honor and glorify Me, because He will take of (receive, draw upon) what is Mine and reveal (declare, disclose, *transmit*) it to you (Amplified, italics mine).

The Holy Spirit will tell you whatever He hears from the Father, and He will glorify Jesus. He may speak directly to your spirit, or He may choose to speak to you through someone else.

Reading and meditating upon God's Word prepares you to recognize and hear the voice of the Holy Spirit by tuning your ears to the true and unchanging tone of the Scriptures. As you tune yourself to the "perfect pitch" of the Spirit, voices or messages containing any mixture of error or deception simply will not ring true. You will recognize the voice of the Spirit as He transmits God's message into your spirit.

Test the Spirits

Since false voices sometimes seek to influence believers, John issued a solemn warning to test the origin of spirits: "Beloved, do not put faith in every spirit, but prove (test) the spirits to discover whether they proceed from God; for many false prophets have gone forth into the world" (1 John 4:1, Amplified).

Demonic voices pretending to be of God sometimes seek to mislead us by speaking lies and deception. Since they speak to us using the same inner frequency that God uses to communicate with us, the origin of their voices can be confusing.

If you have ever been confused or deceived by a lying spirit, you can become "paranoid" and decide to close your ears and shut out any and every voice. But that's like refusing to have a telephone in your house just because you once received an obscene phone call. Spiritual wisdom and discernment are the answer, not spiritual deafness and paranoia.

How do you test the spirits? If you have a spiritual experience that does not line up with the person, nature and character of Jesus Christ, rebuke it and leave it alone because it is of the devil. If you receive a message that does not agree perfectly with the Word of God, disregard it because God never contradicts His Word. (See Ps. 119:4-5,24.) If it doesn't exalt, magnify and glorify Jesus and line up with the eternal purpose of Christ's death, burial and resurrection, forget it. If it brings confusion, condemnation or discouragement, disregard the word because it didn't come from God. (See 1 Cor. 14:33; James 3:15, for example.)

Wait for the Peace of God

If a word seems right and agrees with the Word of God but you have no peace about it, put it on the "back burner" and wait for further guidance from God. Sometimes, even though the word you have heard in your spirit may line up perfectly with the Word of God, it may not be God's will for you or it may not be time to act upon that word. Therefore, learn to let the *presence* or the *absence* of the peace of God in your heart be the determining factor. That is the advice Paul gave Colossian believers:

> And let the peace (soul harmony which comes) from the Christ rule (act as umpire continually) in your hearts— deciding and settling with finality all questions that arise in your minds—[in that peaceful state] to which [as members of Christ's] one body you were also called [to live]... (Col. 3:15, Amplified).

If you were to receive a word that fills your spirit with peace and causes you to break into spontaneous praise and rejoice, don't be afraid to receive it. Satan and your flesh can speak to you and can even quote Scripture, but they cannot counterfeit the peace of God. Peace is a fruit of the Spirit. Satan's "peace" is as hollow and phony as his counterfeits for love or joy. As Paul explained in Colossians 3:15, peace is God's "umpire" that tells us whether a voice, a person or a situation is "safe" or "out." Ultimately, do not act upon the word you have heard unless your heart is filled with God's peace.

Remember this: Satan can try to confuse and mislead you through voices and impressions, but he cannot counterfeit God's deep, settled peace; one of the most accurate tests in the spirit realm is the peace of God.

If You Doubt, Don't

Another way of stating this same principle is: "If you don't know, don't go!" If you don't know if it's God's voice asking you to act, don't step out. If your heart is crowded with lingering doubts and unresolved questions and the peace of God doesn't seem to fall on the situation you're contemplating, maybe God is trying to tell you that a thing is not His will or that something is wrong.

Although Paul wrote Romans 14:23 in reference to another issue (the doctrine of the weaker brother and the eating of meat offered to idols), the principle of acting in faith applies to the doubt and uneasiness we may feel in other situations. Paul said:

> But the man who had doubts—misgivings, an uneasy conscience—about eating, and then eats [perhaps because of you,] stands condemned [before God], because he is not true to his convictions and he does not act from faith. For whatever does not originate and proceed from faith is sin—that is, whatever is done without a conviction of its approval by God is sinful (Amplified).

In other words, if you are not convinced that a thing is right for you, don't do it. You must act from faith, out of your own personal conviction that God approves of your actions. It is sinful to do something just because you hope it's right or because you're imitating someone else.

At Church on the Rock, we emphasize that it should be the Lord who adds members to our church, not some dynamic personality. If the Lord adds people to a church, then He should also be the One to remove them so that they might fulfill His purposes elsewhere. Because we feel this way, we teach our members the importance of seeking the counsel of a member of our pastoral staff before leaving the church to accept tempting job offers or promotions, become members of another church, and so forth.

As a result of this practice, we have been able to lay hands on many choice members and send them out to other churches and ministries with our blessing. Our members have avoided making unwise moves out of a sense of confusion or because of a desire for a different job, a promotion or more money.

I remember the time when one of our members was offered a choice position in a well-known television ministry. The man's sincerity and intense desire for the perfect will of God were immediately evident when he came to me for counsel. He had a heart for ministry and, in the natural, this seemed to be a marvelous opportunity to leave a career he disliked and to channel his energies and talents into full-time ministry.

But, in spite of the fact that he had submitted the matter completely to the lordship of Christ and had taken every step he knew to determine God's will, he could get no peace about dissolving his business, uprooting his family, leaving our church and taking this job.

I must confess that I, too, was puzzled. It seemed like such a fine opportunity. It made sense in the natural. But the peace of God simply refused to fall on it.

After we had prayed and batted the issue around, analyzing it every way we knew how, something clicked in my spirit. I leaned forward, called the man by name and said quietly, "If you don't *know*, don't *go*." He broke into tears, and we knew that we had reached the right decision.

A few years later when the television ministry he had been invited to join was shaken to the core because of immorality, that man and I remembered how the omniscient Spirit of God had blocked a decision that could have resulted in untold hurt and confusion for him. And we thanked God that He really does give His highest and best to those who have hearing ears and obedient hearts.

Regardless of what you have heard some preachers say,

faith is *not* a blind leap in the dark. Faith is a word from the Light. God loves you enough to make His voice unmistakably plain. Don't make a move on any inner directive until all of your doubts and questions, as well as the peace issue, are totally resolved.

Seek Counsel

The Scriptures give frank, clear counsel on many matters. For example, there's no need to pray about whether or not we should withhold our tithes and offerings, commit adultery, forsake the assembling of ourselves together with other believers, tell lies or steal. The Bible clearly forbids such things.

As a matter of fact, if you insist on praying, pleading and badgering God stubbornly to "cut you some slack" and allow you to do something He has expressly forbidden in His Word, you may eventually believe that you have received a yes to your prayers. But there's a catch: God won't have told you to do it. The yes will have come from your own human desires and reasoning or from Satan and his demonic powers.

Face it. The Bible clearly forbids certain things, and we'd better respect those prohibitions. On the other hand, the Bible is silent in regard to some issues.

Therefore, if you can't seem to discern the will of God in certain situations, or if you have some doubt or question in your mind as to what you should or should not do with what you have heard in your spirit, seek the counsel of wise, mature believers.

Second Corinthians 13:1 contains a good principle to remember in seeking the true source of a voice in your spirit: "By the mouth of two or three witnesses every word shall be established." It is easy to be swayed by human desires, personal opinions or emotions. But if you go to two or three mature believers and ask them to seek

God for direction regarding a particular matter of concern, and all of you earnestly pray about the matter, you are not likely to be led astray.

Solomon advised: "Where no wise guidance is, the people fall; but in the multitude of counselors there is safety" (Prov. 11:14, Amplified). He also said: "By wise counsel you can wage your war, and in an abundance of counselors there is victory and safety" (Prov. 24:6, Amplified).

If I hear something that is different, something that is new, even though I have tested it in my spirit, I submit it to godly counselors who will share with me their honest, prayerful opinions.

For instance, when Oral Roberts approached me with the invitation to become dean of the seminary at Oral Roberts University, I wasn't sure what to do. After all, the seminary is in Tulsa, Oklahoma, and my family, home and church are in Rockwall, Texas. So I got down before the Lord and said, "God, You have given me a permanent calling as pastor of Church on the Rock, and I know that I am not to revoke that. I want only Your perfect will in regard to ORU." Then I went back to Oral Roberts and told him the same thing.

Absolutely undaunted, Oral replied, "Larry, you would be of no use at all to this university or to the seminary if you ever stopped pastoring that church. The reason I want you here is that with your hands-on experience, you can teach these preachers how to do the work of the ministry."

I understood exactly what Oral was saying. Some seminaries employ professors who have never won a soul to God, have never preached an effective sermon and have no idea how to pastor a church successfully. Too many seminaries are run by "textbook" scholars who have education but no experience. For many years I had prayed, "Jesus, if You ever give me the chance to train church leaders, I'll try to teach them how to do it right." Knowing that, you can understand why the opportunity Brother Roberts was offering would stir me deeply.

What did I do? I practiced what I preach. I got on my knees and went through the same steps I'm sharing with you. I submitted the entire matter to the lordship of Christ. Because I wanted nothing but His will, I believed with all my heart that God would speak to me. I got very quiet before God and waited for the Holy Spirit to transmit His words, His will, into my spirit. Then I heard His familiar voice: "I have opened a door that no man can close."

To me, that was the word to go ahead and walk through the open door. Wouldn't you have interpreted it that way? But there was a fear in me that I might be misunderstood by our church family if I accepted Oral's invitation. Knowing that I dared not make a mistake in an issue of such vital importance, I went to my church elders, one at a time, and asked for their prayerful counsel. And every one of them said, "This is God."

There are some things in life that are so big, so crucial, that we had better get some godly counsel. But let me emphasize something here. We must be honest with ourselves and with those to whom we go for counsel.

When you need godly advice, don't seek out spiritual "pygmies" who will tell you what you want to hear. Seek out spiritual giants who will counsel you according to the Word of God and the Spirit's leading. Also, be sure to give all the facts to those to whom you go for counsel. Don't hold back vital information or tilt the truth in your favor.

In the end, it all boils down to this: Ask the right people

the right questions and give them the right information. Otherwise, if you try to play games and manipulate, the "counsel" you sought will eventually backfire in your face.

One more word of caution. Sometimes, even after you've honestly sought counsel and desired earnestly to do God's perfect will, some well-meaning people who haven't taken time to seek God's word on the matter may not agree with what God has told you to do—especially if it contradicts their opinions or traditions.

For instance, after it was announced that I would become the dean of the seminary at ORU, one man looked me in the face and said, "If you're going to be the pastor of this church, stay in Rockwall. You put in your eight-to-five right here. That's your job."

I looked right back at him and said, "No, sir. You've got it all wrong. My job is to obey the Spirit of God. If He wants me to go to the North Pole to fast, seek God and live in an igloo for three months, I'll do what He says."

God's ways are not our ways. They may cut across traditions. But if His word to you lines up with the truth of the Scriptures and you know it's a message from Him, go for it!

Wait for God's Timing

Even though we've tried the spirits and used godly counsel to test what we've heard, sometimes that's not enough. We must also wait for God's timing. If there is still not that sure knowledge that we are walking in the very center of God's will, then we must seek God as to His timing.

Some people jump right in and immediately act on the word they have received. But if there is any uncertainty in your spirit after receiving a word from God, always ask, "Lord, when do I do this?"

When Frank and Ann Allen and I saw that the home prayer meetings were off to a healthy start, we talked about starting a church in September 1979. But one day as I was walking across the campus of the seminary from which I was about to graduate, I heard God's voice speak a warning in my spirit: "If you start the church before the first of the year, you will abort this work." That got my attention in a hurry. As a result, we obeyed God and waited until January 1980 to birth the church.

Even nature teaches us that timing is critical. For instance, if a mother tried to bring forth her unborn child four or five months before it was due, that mother and baby would be in a lot of physical trouble. Timing in the spirit world is just as critical.

If God can speak a word to your spirit, He can also tell you when and how to implement that word—in your family, your business, your church. Don't get anxious and run on ahead of God. Wait for His timing.

Obey Boldly

Patience and passivity are not synonymous. Patience (longsuffering) is a godly quality, a fruit of the Spirit. Passivity is the cowardly, apathetic offspring of fear and hopelessness. Therefore, when you know in your spirit that a word is from the Lord and that it is time for you to act upon that word, don't be passive. Step out and obey boldly.

Sometimes you have time to work through some or all of the steps we've talked about before you walk out in obedience. At other times, however, you just sense in your spirit that a thing is right and that it's time to do it. So you ask, "Do You want me to do this right now, Lord?" And He replies, "Yes, right now!" When that happens, go ahead and obey the word you've heard from God.

Let me give you an example of the sort of thing I'm talking about. After graduating from Bible college in 1972, my take-home pay as youth director at Beverly Hills Baptist Church in Dallas was $480 a month. I went to Pastor Howard Conatser and said, "Man, you're paying me too much. I feel bad about taking all this money."

He stared at me, then chuckled and said, "You *are* a young fool, aren't you!" He knew I didn't have any idea what it cost to live.

A few years later, things had changed somewhat. At twenty-eight years of age I was still Pastor Conatser's youth director. But I had a wife and three kids and was making $17,000 a year, whether I was worth it or not.

One Sunday morning the Holy Spirit spoke to me and directed, "If Brother Conatser does anything unusual at all during the time of giving, you give $1,000."

I gulped and said, "Come again, Lord?" I really did. I said, "Now, Lord, let's get this straight." I tried every way in the world to convince myself that I hadn't heard from God, but in my spirit, I knew better.

Sure enough, during the offering, Pastor Conatser stared out over the 3,000 people crowded into the auditorium of the Bronco Bowling Alley in Oak Cliff, where we had moved when the church had outgrown the little building in which we had met, and said: "God is getting ready to do something related to giving in our church, and I don't even know what it is."

Well, it was unusual for him to say anything like that, so before I could talk myself out of it, I jumped to my feet, walked toward him and said, "Pastor, if I'm out of order, sit me down. But God told me to give a thousand dollars."

Always honest and to the point, Brother Conatser turned to me with a grin and said, "Larry, you don't *have* a thousand dollars."

But I was persistent. "The Lord told me to write this check," I insisted. "I've written it, I'm obeying God and that's all I know." Then I turned back to my chair on the platform and sat down.

Before Brother Conatser could turn back around and face the congregation, a spirit of liberality swept over the people. It lasted three-and-a-half hours, from about 10:50 a.m. to 2:30 p.m. People gave cars, boats, lake lots, jewelry, cash, all sorts of things. The cash alone amounted to over $150,000. We tried to tell the people not to give away their stuff, but they insisted. They absolutely refused to take anything back.

Later, our church was written up by the media because of that offering, and some people chose to believe bad things about our pastor and congregation. But the people present in our service that day knew that God had inspired the unusual events. In church that morning, we saw the book of Acts in operation.

I've cautioned you every way I know how to make sure that you've really heard from God. But now I want to make one thing very clear. I'd rather risk looking like a fool and be out there like Peter, walking on the water in obedience to the *rhema* word of the Lord, than to be sitting in the safety of the boat and making fun of people who were trying to walk in the realm of the supernatural. Wouldn't you?

When the time comes that you know in your spirit that there's nothing left to do but obey God, then obey! Don't delay another moment. Do what the Spirit of God is telling you to do. Then leave the results with Him.

Summing It Up

The difference between going on with God and

170

stagnating where you've always been comes down to the matter of hearing and obeying. Don't be like the people of Jeremiah's day. Don't close your ears and rebel against the word of the Lord. Don't hear, then refuse to obey. Hearing is the first step; but obedience is the second. Both steps are necessary to walk with God.

When you hear a voice in your spirit, prevent spiritual blunders and major mistakes by following the simple steps we've just studied. Submit to Christ's lordship and have faith that God will speak to you. Listen as God transmits His word into your spirit. Test the spirits to see if what you have heard lines up with the Scriptures, and wait for the peace of God.

If you've taken these steps and still have doubts, don't force yourself to make a decision one way or the other. Instead, seek the counsel of wise, mature believers. When you're sure that you've heard from God, don't forget to wait for God's timing to act on what you've heard. When the Spirit nudges you and says, "Now's the time," step out and obey boldly.

Personal Growth Activity 9

1. In the past, which of the procedures for determining the will of God has been most difficult for you?
   _____ Submitting the issue to Christ's lordship
   _____ Believing that God will speak to you by His Spirit
   _____ Receiving the message being transmitted
   _____ Testing the spirits
   _____ Waiting for the peace of God
   _____ Refusing to "go" when you didn't "know"
   _____ Seeking and receiving counsel
   _____ Waiting for God's timing
   _____ Obeying boldly

2. If one (or more) of these same problems arises next time you seek to determine God's will, what will you do?

_____

_____

_____

_____

_____

_____

_____

_____

_____

_____

_____

_____

_____

_____

_____

_____

_____

_____

_____

_____

_____

My, What Big Ears
You Have!

O f all the sermons I've ever preached, of all the truths I've ever taught, this message on the hearing ear is the most important. Why? Because it could mean the difference between life or death for you in the days ahead.

Remember the Scripture verse I quoted at the very beginning of this book: "Incline your *ear*, and come to Me. *Hear*, and your soul shall *live*" (Is. 55:3, italics mine)? Receive that word from the Lord. Cherish it. Obey it. It is your very life.

The book of Revelation opens with these words: "The revelation of Jesus Christ, which God gave Him to show His servants—things which must shortly take place" (Rev. 1:1). Then Jesus instructs the apostle John to write specific words of warning and direction to the seven churches in Asia. And to *each* church, one solemn command is repeated: "He who has an *ear*, let him *hear* what the Spirit says to the churches" (italics mine). (See Rev. 2:7,11,17,29; 3:6,13,22.)

Linked with each repeated command to hear what the Spirit says are strong warnings and specific promises. Take a moment to meditate upon the promises in

Revelations 2 and 3 that God spoke to overcoming believers who have hearing ears.

> He who has an ear, let him hear what the Spirit says to the churches. To him who overcomes I will give to eat from the tree of life, which is in the midst of the Paradise of God (2:7).
>
> He who overcomes shall not be hurt by the second death (2:11).
>
> I will give some of the hidden manna to eat. And I will give him a white stone, and on the stone a new name written which no one knows except him who receives it (2:17).
>
> And he who overcomes, and keeps My works until the end to him I will give power over the nations...and I will give him the morning star (2:26,28).
>
> He who overcomes shall be clothed in white garments, and I will not blot out his name from the Book of Life; but I will confess his name before My Father and before His angels (3:5).
>
> ...I will make him a pillar in the temple of My God, and he shall go out no more. And I will write on him the name of my God and the name of the city of My God....And I will write on him My new name (3:12).
>
> To him who overcomes I will grant to sit with Me on My throne, as I also overcame and sat down with My Father on His throne (3:21).

In Revelation 3:20, Jesus declares, "Behold, I stand at the door, and knock: if anyone *hears* My voice and opens the door, I will come in to him and dine with him, and he with Me." Then for the seventh time, Jesus commands: "He who has an *ear*, let him *hear* what the Spirit says to the churches" (3:22, italics mine).

I don't understand all the wonder and power contained in the promises God made to believers who hear His voice. A "white stone," the "hidden manna" and a "new name" sound foreign and strange to me, just as references to "lasers," "satellites," "computers" and "access codes" would not have been fully comprehended or appreciated by people living a century ago. But I certainly understand what Jesus meant when He talked about *hearing ears* and *life or death*. Don't you?

As this century draws to a close, once again Jesus is giving His church a choice. Christians have a decision to make. We can get down to business with God and get busy developing hearing ears, or we can ignore His warning, go on our merry way and get nullified and annihilated.

If you want to be a survivor, if you plan to be one of those overcomers that Jesus talked about, prayer must become a dialogue, a conversation. Instead of hearing God only through others—from the outside in, you must hear Him speak directly to you, from the inside out. You must become intimately acquainted with His voice and His ways.

But that's not all. As you develop hearing ears, you must obey God's voice boldly and walk in His wise counsel, trusting His sure, steady hand to guide all you do.

Forget about learning to cope with failure. Stop coping and start winning! If you're tired of getting your second orders, if you've had it "up to here" with being out of the will of God, get busy and develop hearing ears. The Spirit of God will lead you into paths of victory, peace and safety.

Do you long to be a radical, dynamic Christian who

lives and walks in the supernatural realm of the Spirit? It all starts by praying, "God, help me develop ears that hear the voice of Your Spirit. Grace me with the ability to hear and the boldness to obey."

We've talked about how to hear and know God's voice. Now it's up to you. Don't delay any longer. Take your next step. Decide to be an overcomer. Choose life, not death. Start developing those big "Mickey Mouse" hearing ears!

Notes

Chapter 1

1. See James Robison, *Thank God, I'm Free* (Nashville, Tenn.: Thomas Nelson Publishers, 1988).

Chapter 2

1. John Wimber with Kevin Springer, *Power Evangelism* (San Francisco: Harper & Row, 1986), pp. 32-35.

Chapter 6

1. Harold Horton, *The Gifts of the Spirit* (Springfield, Mo.: Gospel Publishing House, reprint 1975), pp. 148,149.

Chapter 7

1. Bilquis Sheikh with Richard H. Schneider, *I Dared to Call Him Father* (Old Tappan, N.J.: Chosen Books, 1978), pp. 46-53.
2. C.M. Ward, *Revivaltime Pulpit*, sermon book number 4 (Springfield, Mo.: Assemblies of God National Radio Department, 1960), pp. 77-79.
3. Gordon Lindsay, *Prayer That Moves Mountains* (Dallas: Christ for the Nations Inc., reprint 1984), pp. 47,48.

Chapter 8

1. Loren Cunningham with Janice Rogers, *Is That Really You, God?* (Old Tappan, N.J.: Chosen Books, 1984), pp. 19,20.
2. Ibid., pp. 20-22.